THE LITTLE BOOK OF
baking

55 Homemade Cookies, Cakes, Cupcakes & Pies to Make & Share

Brown Sugar and Pecan Fingers (recipe page 51)

Good Housekeeping

THE LITTLE BOOK OF
baking

**55 Homemade Cookies, Cakes,
Cupcakes & Pies to Make & Share**

HEARST BOOKS
New York

HEARST BOOKS
New York

An Imprint of Sterling Publishing
387 Park Avenue South
New York, NY 10016

ISBN 978-1-58816-972-3

Good Housekeeping
ROSEMARY ELLIS
Editor in Chief

COURTNEY MURPHY
Creative Director

SUSAN WESTMORELAND
Food Director

SAMANTHA B. CASSETTY, MS, RD
Nutrition Director

SHARON FRANKE
Kitchen Appliances & Food Technology Director

Book design by Amy Sly & Laura Palese
Project editor: Sarah Scheffel
Photography credits on page 128

The Good Housekeeping Cookbook Seal guarantees that the recipes in this cookbook meet the strict standards of the Good Housekeeping Research Institute. The Institute has been a source of reliable information and a consumer advocate since 1900, and established its seal of approval in 1909. Every recipe has been triple-tested for ease, reliability, and great taste.

Distributed in Canada by Sterling Publishing
C/o Canadian Manda Group,
165 Dufferin Street
Toronto, Ontario, Canada M6K 3H6
Distributed in the United Kingdom by GMC Distribution Services
Castle Place, 166 High Street, Lewes, East Sussex, England BN7 1XU
Distributed in Australia by Capricorn Link (Australia) Pty. Ltd.
P.O. Box 704, Windsor, NSW 2756, Australia

For information about custom editions, special sales, and premium and corporate purchases, please contact Sterling Special Sales at 800-805-5489 or specialsales@sterlingpublishing.com.

Manufactured in China

10 9 8 7 6 5 4 3 2 1

www.sterlingpublishing.com

contents

Lemon Bars (recipe page 44)

Foreword

Do you remember the first thing you ever baked? Holiday sugar cookies that you cut out and decorated with your mom? Or maybe it was brownies, a project devised by your babysitter to distract you from missing your parents. For me it was shaping biscotti logs with my grandmother.

I have especially fond memories of those lopsided logs, and my sweet tooth has insured that "my life in baked goods" now includes myriad, cookies, cakes, and pies, many of which I make again and again. Happily for me, *The Little Book of Baking* compiles many of these classics—from a down-home deep-dish apple pie to a rich chocolate layer cake—along with new favorite things. The nostalgia-steeped recipe for Hermit Bars was the hit of my son's school snack repertoire, while the Rich Chocolate Cupcakes got one of his first-grade classmates to declare, "These are the best cupcakes I've had in my whole life." To wow guests with a decadent chocolate dessert, I often serve Warm Chocolate Soufflé Cakes or the Chocolate Caramel Walnut Tart, topped with dollops of whipped cream. And my freezer usually sports a few logs of cookie dough—the Lemon Slice-'n'-Bake cookie dough is a no-brainer, but the double chocolate chip, gingery snickerdoodles, and oatmeal-chocolate cherry doughs are all great freeze-and-bake options, too.

The Little Book of Baking provides you with these yummy recipes and many more, plus tips on making perfect cookies and bars, cakes and cupcakes, pies and tarts that'll help even a beginner baker turn out irresistible treats. From rolling out delectable piecrust to creating whimsical cupcakes, you will learn to become a better baker. We hope this book will encourage you to enjoy the simple pleasures of baking—and eating the results!

—Susan Westmoreland
Food Director, *Good Housekeeping*

Double Fruit Pies (recipe page 90)

baking basics

Crisp or chewy cookies, pretty frosted cupcakes, luscious pies and tarts—recipes for all of these are at your fingertips in *The Little Book of Baking*. For best results, before you begin, take a few minutes to peruse the following secrets to successful baking. In addition, see our tips at the beginning of each chapter (pages 24, 56, and 88).

START WITH THE RIGHT INGREDIENTS

To ensure that your baked goods will taste delicious and have just the right texture, it is important to use the exact ingredients called for and to handle them properly.

* **Butter vs. margarine.** When a recipe calls for butter or margarine, we prefer salted butter. Do not substitute margarine for butter if a recipe does not list it as an option. For those recipes that do, if you prefer to use margarine, make sure it contains 80 percent fat. Don't substitute light margarine or vegetable-oil spreads for stick margarine, and don't use whipped butter, either. Those products contain more water than standard sticks and won't work in baked goods unless the recipes have been formulated especially for them.

* **To soften butter or margarine,** let it stand wrapped on a counter or unwrapped in a mixing bowl, at room temperature for an hour. You can speed up the process by cutting it into small pieces first. If you're in a hurry, the idea of popping cold butter or margarine into the microwave can be tempting, but the Test Kitchen has found that zapping butter either softens it unevenly by creating hot spots, or melts it in a blink. Butter that is melted or nearly melted will be too soft to cream properly, and will affect the texture of the finished baked goods.

* **The type of flour is important.** Most of these recipes call for all-purpose flour. Occasionally, a recipe will call for cake flour, which is higher in starch and will produce a more tender cake or treat. Cake

and all-purpose flours are not interchangeable, so use the type of flour specified in the ingredients list. In either case, make sure the flour you are using is *not* self-rising.

* **Baking soda vs. baking powder.** Both products are leavening agents—they make baked goods rise. Baking powder is a premeasured mixture of baking soda and an acid. (It takes twice as much baking powder as baking soda to leaven a product.) Do not substitute baking soda for baking powder or vice versa. Store both products tightly closed in their original box or tin, in a cool, dry place so they stay active. For best results, replace baking soda and baking powder after six months if you haven't used them up.

* **To test whether baking soda is still active,** combine a teaspoonful with white vinegar; if it froths up immediately and vigorously, it's active. To test whether baking powder is still active, stir a teaspoonful into a cup of hot tap water. If the water bubbles vigorously, it's still fresh. In the case of both baking soda and powder, delayed, little, or no bubbling means the leavener is past its prime.

TOASTING NUTS

An easy way to make your cookies, cakes, and pies taste even better is to toast the nuts called for in the recipe—this makes them more flavorful. Toast nuts whole and let them cool before chopping them, if that's specified in the recipe. These instructions work for toasting walnuts, pecans, almonds, macadamia nuts, and hazelnuts.

* Preheat the oven to 350°F and position the rack in the middle. (If you aren't already heating the oven for baking, you can use a toaster oven instead.)

* Spread out the nuts in a single layer on a rimmed baking pan such as a jelly-roll pan.

* Bake until the nuts are lightly browned, 10 to 15 minutes, stirring occasionally so the nuts in the center of the pan circulate to the edges, where they will brown faster.

* Immediately transfer the nuts to a cool platter or baking pan to reduce their temperature and stop the browning. To remove the bitter skins from hazelnuts, see the tip below.

* If you're toasting just a few nuts, heat them in a dry skillet over low heat for 3 to 5 minutes, stirring frequently.

TIP Toast hazelnuts as directed above until fragrant and any portions without skin begin to brown. Transfer the nuts to a clean, dry kitchen towel and rub them until the skins come off.

KNOW YOUR CHOCOLATE AND COCOA

Here's a guide to the types of chocolate you'll find in our recipes. You don't have to blow your budget by buying a super-premium brand, but don't skimp on quality either.

* **cocoa powder** There are two types of unsweetened cocoa, alkalized (Dutch-processed) and nonalkalized (natural). Dutch-processed cocoa is treated with an alkali to neutralize its acidity, which creates a darker but less intensely flavored cocoa. We use natural cocoa in our recipes. Look closely at the label when buying cocoa; some are alkalized even if the label doesn't say "Dutch-processed." Do not be tempted to substitute instant cocoa mix for unsweetened cocoa.

* **unsweetened chocolate** This is ground cocoa beans (called chocolate liquor) in solid form with no sugar added. It's sold in packages of 1-ounce squares.

* **bittersweet chocolate** Chocolate that has not been sweetened. The higher the level of chocolate liquor it contains, the less sweet it will be. Available in bars, packages of 1-ounce squares, and chips.

* **semisweet chocolate** This type of chocolate contains more sugar than bittersweet chocolate. It is available in bars, packages of 1-ounce squares, and chips.

* **sweet chocolate** This dark baking chocolate is usually sold under a brand name (and used to make recipes like our German Chocolate Brownies). Do not confuse it with bitter- or semisweet chocolate. It can be found in the baking aisle in most grocery stores.

* **white chocolate** Chocolate in name only (it contains no chocolate liquor), white chocolate is vanilla-flavored sweetened cocoa butter (a byproduct of chocolate processing). Although some brands substitute vegetable oil for the cocoa butter, for the best quality, look for a brand that contains cocoa butter.

HANDLING CHOCOLATE

* **melting chocolate** All types of chocolate should be melted in a double boiler over low heat to prevent scorching. Alternatively, place the chocolate in a microwave-safe bowl and microwave at 50 percent power, stirring at intervals. To speed melting, chop the chocolate into small pieces and stir frequently.

* **storing chocolate** Store chocolate, well wrapped, in a cool, dark place (65°F is ideal). If storage conditions are too cold, chocolate will "sweat" when brought to room temperature. If conditions are too warm, the cocoa will start to melt, and a gray "bloom" will form on the surface. This doesn't affect the flavor of the chocolate.

THE RIGHT EQUIPMENT FOR THE JOB

Below is an overview of basic baking equipment. Read through each recipe to make sure you have the right pans and tools on hand before you begin.

* **mixing** You may be tempted to stir up your batter or dough with a spoon snatched in haste from your drawer, but using the right mixing equipment makes it easier, particularly if your dough is thick or includes a lot of add-ins like nuts. You'll appreciate the power of a heavy-duty stand mixer or handheld mixer and a food

processor or mini processor. And you definitely need a set of mixing bowls (small, medium, and large); wooden spoons for stirring hot ingredients; and a rubber spatula for scraping down the sides of the bowls. A whisk comes in handy for beating items like eggs and cream.

* **baking** Use the pan type and dimensions called for in each recipe, whether that's a cookie sheet, round baking pans for a layer cake, ramekins, or a pie plate. We like heavy-gauge aluminum pans and cookie sheets. Because they are thick, they prevent overbrowning. If your cookie sheets or pans are old and discolored, you can line them with foil to help deflect the heat. You'll need a cooling rack to ensure good air circulation after your baked goods come out of the oven, and a wide metal spatula for transferring cookies from sheet to rack. For some of our tart recipes, we recommend a tart pan with a removable bottom; it will allow you to easily remove your finished tart from the pan. If you have a standard tart pan, simply slice and serve after cooling.

* **decorating** Baking supply stores carrying enough decorating supplies to fill every shelf in your kitchen, and it would be a pleasure to own them all! But to doll up the baked goods in this book, here's all you'll need: some cookie cutters (heart-shaped if you want to make our Lemon Hearts on page 34), a pastry bag and tips (or simply fill a zip-tight bag with frosting, snip off ⅛ inch of one corner, and squeeze), and an offset spatula for frosting cupcakes and cakes.

GETTING STARTED

Baking is fun, but it also requires careful attention to detail: You have to choose the right pan size, measure accurately, heat the oven to the correct temperature, and remember to remove your treats from the oven at the correct time! Here are four basic rules of baking to help get you on your way:

* **Get to know the recipe.** Before you start measuring ingredients, read the recipe all the way through. Butter may have to be softened, nuts may need to be toasted, chocolate may need to be melted.

* **Gather your ingredients.** Assemble everything you need from the pantry and refrigerator, and group them into dry ingredients and wet ingredients. Be sure to soften butter or margarine to room temperature (68° to 70°F) if the recipe calls for it. This can take up to an hour, so plan ahead (see page 9 for details).

* **No swapping.** Don't plan on using a substitute for any of the ingredients unless one is specifically offered in the recipe.

* **Measure everything.** In baking, adding a pinch of this and a dash of that can lead to disaster. Recipes for baked goods are exact formulas, and what you add—or subtract—can adversely affect the taste and texture of the finished product. For foolproof results, review our instructions for measuring dry and wet ingredients below.

MEASURING BY MEASURE

To get the same results every time you make a recipe, whether you're baking cookies, cakes, or pies, you must use standard measuring equipment and take the time to measure with care. Even though it worked for Grandma, don't use tableware teaspoons and tablespoons or coffee or teacups for measuring.

Always use measuring spoons to measure both liquid and dry ingredients. For convenience, measure the dry ingredients first, so the spoons remain dry until it's time to move on to the wet ingredients. Use stackable dry ingredient cups to measure dry ingredients; clear cups with spouts for liquids. Never use dry-ingredient cups to measure liquid ingredients or liquid-ingredient cups to measure dry ingredients. And always measure ingredients over waxed paper or into an empty bowl, rather than over your bowl of already measured ingredients—just in case there is a spill.

Follow these tips on measuring common baking ingredients:

* **baking soda and powder** Use a clean, dry measuring spoon and level it off with a spatula or knife.

* **flour** To measure flour, which tends to pack down in its storage container, stir and then spoon it into a standard-sized dry-ingredient measuring cup. Level the top with a spatula or the back of a knife, scraping the excess into a bowl. Never scoop the flour directly from the canister or package of flour; the flour will become packed down and you'll end up adding more than is called for. See Measuring Flour, opposite, for photos of the process.

* **sugar** Just scoop or pour *granulated sugar* into a dry-ingredient measuring cup, then level the top with the back of a knife. *Confectioners' sugar* should be sifted before measuring to break up clumps. Lightly spoon the sifted sugar into the measuring cup and then level. To measure *brown sugar*, pack it into the measuring cup and then level. Don't use a larger cup than is needed for the sugar and attempt to eyeball the quantity.

* **nuts** If the recipe calls for *1 cup walnuts, chopped,* measure whole walnuts, then chop them. If it calls for *1 cup chopped walnuts,* chop and then measure. The quantities won't be the same!

* **butter, margarine, and vegetable shortening** Tablespoons are marked on the wrapper, so you can just cut off the desired amount using a knife. One stick of butter contains 8 tablespoons or ½ cup.

MEASURING FLOUR

STEP 1 Stir the flour to keep it from packing and scoop it into a standard dry measuring cup.

STEP 2 Level the top of the flour by passing the back of a knife or a metal spatula across the cup to remove excess flour.

* **liquids** When measuring liquid ingredients, use a clear measuring cup with a spout. Place the cup on a level surface and bend down so that your eyes are in line with the marks on the cup. For *maple syrup, honey, and other sticky liquids,* if you lightly oil the measuring cup first, the syrup will pour right out without sticking to it.

* **cookie dough** For the best results, make all cookies the same size. If you bake a lot, invest in a cookie scoop with a trigger handle for easy release of dough onto the cookie sheet.

MIXING DOUGHS AND BATTERS

How you mix the dough affects the outcome of the finished baked goods.

* **Know your electric mixer.** If your mixer is a powerful stand type, you may not need to mix the ingredients for the full amount of time indicated in the recipes. If your model has less power or is the hand-held type, you may need to mix longer. To make it easy, recipes describe what the dough or batter should look like when it's fully mixed, as well as timings to achieve the best results.

* **Frequently scrape the side of the bowl.** Use a rubber spatula—a metal spoon won't clean the side as well and could cause airy batters to deflate.

* **Overmixing results in tough baked goods.** Unless otherwise specified, after adding the flour, mix the dough only until blended.

PICKS AND PANS

Selecting the appropriate pan and greasing it to prevent your baked goods from sticking are among the keys to success. See the Pan Volumes chart (page 121) for a list of standard pan sizes.

* **Use the pan size called for in the recipe.** For example, don't substitute an 8-inch pan for a 9-inch pan or vice versa. The bake time given in each recipe is based on specific bakeware dimensions. Some pans have dimensions printed on the bottom. If yours doesn't, see Measuring Pans (page 121) for tips on calculating the volume.

* **Prepare the pan before you mix the batter.** That way, it's ready to go when the batter is mixed. If you grease the pan after mixing the batter, the leavening agents might start to work too early, or in the case of egg-rich batters, volume will decrease, which will affect the baked item.

* **For best results, grease pans with vegetable shortening.**
You can also use nonstick cooking spray—spritz lightly so it doesn't bead up. Greasing with butter creates a nice golden-brown crust, but the baked goods are more likely to stick to the pan. Some recipes for sticky goodies call for lining the pan with parchment paper. For cookies and pastries, reusable silicone baking mats are handy. Just place them on the cookie sheet before scooping the dough; no greasing required—then wash in warm soapy water after using.

KEEP TABS ON TIME AND TEMPERATURE

You don't want to either underbake or overbake. This is especially important with cookies, which often are exposed to a high temperature for a short period of time. That's why it's crucial to have an accurate gauge of your oven's temperature. If you aren't sure whether your oven is properly calibrated, buy a good oven thermometer and place it on the center rack in the center of the oven. Once you've set the temperature, allow 15 minutes for the oven to fully preheat, confirm that you've reached the desired heat level, make any necessary adjustments, and then put your pan or cookie sheet in the oven.

* **Timing is too important** to count on your ability to keep an eye on the clock. It's easy to get distracted, and in baking, just a few minutes can mean the difference between an irresistible golden-brown top and charred baked goods that end up in the trash. A kitchen timer is a worthy investment. Another good investment: two sturdy pot holders. If you use a kitchen towel, you or the towel may get burned.

* **Set a kitchen timer for the shortest baking time** in the range stated in the recipe. If your baked goods aren't done at that point, watch them carefully for the remainder of the time to avoid overbaking. Resist the temptation to open the oven door to check on them. The temperature will drop, and they may not rise properly. Rely on an oven light, if you have one, or check again when the treats reach the upper end of the baking time specified in the recipe.

STORING YOUR BAKED GOODS

To keep your treats fresh, cool them thoroughly, then follow these storage tips.

* **cookies and bars** Store cookies in airtight containers and remember that not every cookie can survive in a cookie jar: Choose cookies that are sturdy enough to withstand a big cookie pileup without crumbling or smooshing. Most cookies can be stored at room temperature, but to keep them longer, you may wish to freeze them. To do this, place them in airtight containers cushioned with crumpled waxed paper for a secure fit. For decorated cookies, freeze them in a single layer on a cookie sheet until they are hard, then pack them for storage, separating the layers with waxed paper. Store brownies and bar cookies (cut or uncut) in the baking pan, covered with a layer of plastic wrap or foil. You can also freeze them for up to three months. First, wrap the bars in several layers of plastic or foil, then place them in a freezer-weight bag.

* **cakes and cupcakes** Store sheet cakes in the baking pan covered with a layer of plastic wrap or foil. For layer cakes, you will need a cake keeper for the finished cake. Alternatively, you can hold off on assembly: Wrap the individual layers in plastic, then build and frost the cake when you are ready to serve it. Many cakes are best kept at room temperature, but always refrigerate cheesecakes and cakes that contain fillings or frostings made with whipped cream, cream cheese, sour cream, yogurt, or eggs. For maximum freshness, cupcakes should be stored in an airtight container with a lid. To freeze butter cakes, wrap them in plastic then in heavy-duty foil or a freezer-weight zip-tight bag.

* **pies and tarts** Fruit pies can be covered and stored overnight at room temperature. For longer storage, refrigerate. Meringue pies are best the day they are made. Pies with cream or custard filling should be refrigerated as soon as they cool. Refrigerate any leftovers.

Chocolate Almond Meringues (recipe page 40)

cookies & bars

BAKE THE BEST COOKIES EVER!

Some of the easiest treats to create, cookies are often the first baking projects chosen by kids and novice bakers alike. To ensure successful results, take a few minutes to read our tips before you begin. Then try your hand at our fast and easy Warm Chocolate Chunk Pizza Cookie or our basic but beloved Butterscotch Blondies or Hermit Bars.

* When dropping, shaping, or rolling and cutting dough, try to maintain a uniform size and thickness to ensure even baking. Follow directions exactly for the amount of dough used per cookie. If a recipe says "drop by rounded teaspoons," we mean measuring teaspoons, not spoons used to stir tea. A 1-inch ball should really be an inch in diameter—measure one to get the idea.

* When making sugar cookies or other rolled treats, work on a flat surface. Roll from the center to the edge and cut as many cookies as possible from each rolling (rerolled scraps make tougher cookies).

* Cookies won't brown evenly in jelly-roll pans. Make sure to use a flat cookie sheet (the type with a lip on one end will help you grip it). For proper heat distribution, sheets should be at least 2 inches smaller on all sides than your oven. Arrange oven rack in center position if you are baking one sheet at a time.

* To speed things up (and avoid having to clean between batches), line sheets with parchment paper or a silicone liner. As the first batch bakes, set up additional parchment or silicone with dough so it is ready to slide onto the sheet or sheets.

* Cool cookie sheets between batches. Dough placed on hot metal will spread before it's in the oven, making for pancake-flat cookies.

* Down to the last batch with enough dough for only half a sheet? Spread out cookies evenly; a half-empty cookie sheet can warp.

BAR TENDING

Although bars are the simplest type of cookies to bake, they must be sliced and stored with care.

Allow bars to cool completely before cutting or storing. Don't cover or wrap warm bar cookies—the heat will cause condensation, making the tops wet and gummy.

Cut bars with a sharp chef's knife, using a gentle sawing motion. This will prevent jagged edges, broken pieces, and squashed sides. For fudgy, frosted, or cheesecake-style bars, dip the knife blade into hot water, then quickly dry it with a paper towel before each cut. This will help keep the bars from sticking to your knife.

Store uncut bars at room temperature in the baking pan you made them in; cover with a layer of plastic wrap and foil. You can also freeze bars for up to three months; use several layers of plastic wrap or foil and place the bars in freezer-weight plastic bags.

double chocolate chip cookies

This new take on America's most popular cookie combines semisweet and white chocolate chips for a delicious double-chocolate sensation.

active time 30 minutes   **bake time** 10 minutes per batch
makes about 24 cookies

1½ cups all-purpose flour

½ cup butter (1 stick), softened (no substitutions)

¾ cup packed brown sugar

¼ cup granulated sugar

2½ teaspoons vanilla extract

½ teaspoon baking soda

¼ teaspoon salt

1 large egg

¾ cup semisweet chocolate chips

¾ cup white chocolate chips

each cookie About 160 calories, 2g protein, 21g carbohydrate, 8g total fat (5g saturated), 1g fiber, 21mg cholesterol, 105mg sodium

1 Preheat oven to 375°F.

2 Into large bowl, measure flour, butter, sugars, vanilla, baking soda, salt, and egg. With mixer on medium speed, beat until blended and smooth, occasionally scraping bowl with rubber spatula. With wooden spoon, stir in all chocolate chips.

3 Drop dough by rounded tablespoons, 2 inches apart, onto two ungreased large cookie sheets. Bake until golden, 10 to 12 minutes, rotating cookies sheets between upper and lower oven racks halfway through. Immediately transfer cookies to wire racks to cool.

warm chocolate chunk pizza cookie

Enjoy this slice-of-heaven cookie warm—just minutes out of the oven. Or bake it ahead and heat up as many wedges as you like just before serving.

active time 15 minutes **bake time** 20 minutes
makes 16 wedges

1 Preheat oven to 375°F. Grease large cookie sheet. On waxed paper, combine flour, baking soda, and salt.

2 In 3-quart saucepan, melt butter over medium heat. Remove from heat. With wire whisk, stir in sugars, vanilla, and egg until mixed. With wooden spoon, stir in flour mixture just until blended. Stir in chocolate and walnuts.

3 Spoon batter onto center of prepared cookie sheet and, with rubber spatula, flatten and spread into 8-inch round. Bake until cookie is golden brown, 20 to 23 minutes. Cool on wire rack 5 minutes, then cut into 16 wedges and serve. Or cool completely and wrap in foil; to serve warm, reheat in 375°F oven 5 to 8 minutes.

1 cup all-purpose flour

½ teaspoon baking soda

¼ teaspoon salt

6 tablespoons butter or margarine

⅓ cup granulated sugar

⅓ cup packed brown sugar

1 teaspoon vanilla extract

1 large egg

6 ounces semisweet chocolate, broken into small pieces

½ cup walnuts, coarsely chopped

each wedge About 170 calories, 2g protein, 20g carbohydrate, 10g total fat (5g saturated), 1g fiber, 25mg cholesterol, 126mg sodium

chocolate cherry oatmeal cookies

For chewy cookies, bake these for the minimum time—for a crispy treat, bake them a few minutes longer.

active time 35 minutes   **bake time** 12 minutes per batch
makes about 54 cookies

1½ cups all-purpose flour

2 teaspoons baking soda

½ teaspoon salt

¾ cup granulated sugar

¾ cup packed brown sugar

¾ cup butter or margarine (1½ sticks), softened

2 teaspoons vanilla extract

2 large eggs

3 cups old-fashioned oats, uncooked

1 cup dried tart cherries or dark seedless raisins

1 cup semisweet chocolate chips (6 ounces)

each cookie About 100 calories, 1g protein, 15g carbohydrate, 4g total fat (2g saturated), 1g fiber, 15mg cholesterol, 100mg sodium

1 Preheat oven to 350°F. Grease large cookie sheet.

2 On waxed paper, combine flour, baking soda, and salt.

3 In large bowl, with mixer on medium speed, beat sugars and butter until creamy, occasionally scraping bowl with rubber spatula. Beat in vanilla, then eggs, one at a time, beating well after each. On low speed, gradually beat in flour mixture just until blended, occasionally scraping bowl with spatula. With wooden spoon, stir in oats, dried fruit, and chocolate chips.

4 Drop dough by rounded measuring tablespoons, 2 inches apart, onto two prepared cookie sheets. Bake until tops are golden, 12 to 14 minutes, rotating cookie sheets between upper and lower oven racks halfway through. Transfer cookies to wire racks to cool completely. Repeat with remaining dough.

lemon slice-'n'-bakes

Recipes like this one, which calls for cookie dough to be chilled, then sliced, started appearing after the arrival of the electric refrigerator in the 1930s.

active time 25 minutes plus chilling **bake time** 13 minutes per batch
makes about 64 cookies

2 cups all-purpose flour

¼ teaspoon baking soda

¼ teaspoon salt

2 large lemons

¾ cup butter or margarine (1½ sticks), softened

½ cup confectioners' sugar

½ cup plus 2 tablespoons granulated sugar

½ teaspoon vanilla extract

each cookie About 40 calories, 0g protein, 5g carbohydrate, 2g total fat (1g saturated), 0g fiber, 6mg cholesterol, 35mg sodium

1 On waxed paper, combine flour, baking soda, and salt. From lemons, grate 1 tablespoon peel and squeeze 2 tablespoons juice.

2 In large bowl, with mixer on medium speed, beat butter, confectioners' sugar, and ½ cup granulated sugar until creamy. Add vanilla and lemon peel and juice; beat until blended. On low speed, beat in flour mixture just until combined.

3 Divide dough in half. Shape each half into 6-inch-long log. Wrap each log in waxed paper and refrigerate overnight. (If using margarine, freeze logs overnight.)

4 Preheat oven to 350°F. Remove 1 log from refrigerator and cut into 3/16-inch-thick slices. Place slices, 1½ inches apart, on two ungreased large cookie sheets. Sprinkle lightly with some of remaining granulated sugar.

5 Bake until edges are golden brown, 13 to 14 minutes, rotating cookie sheets between upper and lower oven racks halfway through. Cool on cookie sheets on wire racks 2 minutes. Transfer cookies to racks to cool completely. Repeat with remaining dough and granulated sugar.

SHAPING AND SLICING
ICEBOX COOKIES

After wrapping the dough log, feel free to freeze it until you're ready to bake some cookies.

STEP 1 Shape the dough roughly into a log, then use a sheet of waxed paper to roll and smooth it into a cylinder of even thickness. Twist the ends of the waxed paper to seal.

STEP 2 As you slice the log of dough, turn it every few cuts so that one side doesn't become flattened.

pb and j thumbprints

Here's the perfect choice for kids who love peanut butter and jelly sandwiches.

active time 45 minutes   bake time 13 minutes per batch
makes about 48 cookies

1½ cups all-purpose flour

½ teaspoon baking powder

¼ teaspoon baking soda

⅛ teaspoon salt

½ cup butter or margarine (1 stick), softened

½ cup creamy peanut butter

½ cup packed brown sugar

¼ cup granulated sugar

1 large egg

1 tablespoon dark corn syrup

1 teaspoon vanilla extract

⅔ cup dry-roasted peanuts, finely chopped

⅓ cup strawberry jam

each cookie About 70 calories, 1g protein, 9g carbohydrate, 4g total fat (1g saturated), 8mg cholesterol, 55mg sodium

1 Preheat oven to 350°F. In medium bowl, whisk flour, baking powder, baking soda, and salt.

2 In large bowl, with mixer on medium speed, beat butter, peanut butter, and sugars until creamy, occasionally scraping bowl with rubber spatula. Add egg, corn syrup, and vanilla; beat until well blended. Reduce speed to low; gradually beat in flour mixture just until blended, occasionally scraping bowl.

3 On waxed paper, place peanuts. Shape dough by rounded measuring teaspoons into 1-inch balls; roll in peanuts. Place balls, 2 inches apart, on two ungreased large cookie sheets. With thumb or end of wooden spoon handle, make small indentation in center of each ball.

4 Bake 8 minutes, rotating cookie sheets between upper and lower oven racks halfway through. Remove cookies from oven and press each indentation again; fill each with rounded ¼ teaspoon jam. Continue baking until cookies are set and edges begin to brown, 5 to 6 minutes longer. Transfer cookies to wire racks to cool. Repeat with remaining dough, peanuts, and jam.

ginger-spiced snickerdoodles

We added aromatic spices to these crackly New England treats.

active time 30 minutes   **bake time** 12 minutes per batch
makes about 42 cookies

1 Preheat oven to 375°F. In medium bowl, whisk flour, cream of tartar, baking soda, ginger, cinnamon, and salt.

2 In large bowl, with mixer on medium speed, beat granulated sugar with butter until creamy, occasionally scraping bowl with rubber spatula. Beat in molasses, vanilla, and egg. At low speed, gradually add flour mixture just until blended, occasionally scraping bowl.

3 With hands, shape dough by rounded tablespoons into 1½-inch balls. Roll balls in coarse sugar to coat. Place balls, 2 inches apart, on two ungreased large cookie sheets.

4 Bake cookies 12 to 14 minutes or until lightly golden and crinkly on top, rotating cookie sheets between upper and lower oven racks halfway through. Set cookie sheets on wire racks for 1 minute to cool slightly, then transfer cookies to racks to cool completely.

5 Repeat with remaining dough and coarse sugar.

3¼ cups all-purpose flour

2 teaspoons cream of tartar

1 teaspoon baking soda

1 teaspoon ground ginger

1 teaspoon ground cinnamon

½ teaspoon salt

1⅓ cups granulated sugar

1 cup butter or margarine (2 sticks), softened

¼ cup light (mild) molasses

1 teaspoon vanilla extract

1 large egg

½ cup coarse sugar (see Tip)

each cookie About 115 calories, 1g protein, 17g carbohydrate, 5g total fat (3g saturated), 0g fiber, 18mg cholesterol, 105mg sodium

TIP Coarse (or decorating) sugar has granules about four times larger than granulated sugar. It can be found in baking-supply stores.

lemon hearts

These delicately glazed heart-shaped cookies make a charming gift. Package them in a box or tin with waxed paper between each layer.

active time 40 minutes plus cooling   bake time 15 minutes per batch
makes about 72 cookies

2 lemons

3 cups all-purpose flour

3 tablespoons cornstarch

¾ teaspoon salt

1½ cups butter (3 sticks), softened (no substitutions)

2½ cups confectioners' sugar

1½ teaspoons lemon extract

¼ teaspoon almond extract

1 Preheat oven to 325°F. From lemons, grate 4½ teaspoons peel and squeeze 5 teaspoons juice; set aside.

2 In medium bowl, whisk flour, cornstarch, and salt until blended. In large bowl, with mixer on medium speed, beat butter and 1 cup confectioners' sugar until creamy, occasionally scraping bowl with rubber spatula. Beat in 1 tablespoon lemon peel and both extracts. Reduce speed to low; gradually beat in flour mixture until blended, occasionally scraping bowl.

3 Divide dough in half. Between two 20-inch sheets of waxed paper, roll 1 dough half ⅜ inch thick. (If paper wrinkles, peel it off, gently pull to remove wrinkles, and reposition.) With floured 2¼-inch heart-shaped cutter, cut out as many cookies as possible. With floured ¾-inch heart-shaped cutter, cut out and remove centers from cookies. Reserve centers and trimmings to reroll.

4 With lightly floured spatula, place cookies, 1 inch apart, on two ungreased large cookie sheets. (If dough gets too soft to transfer to sheet, freeze for about 10 minutes.)

5 Bake cookies until edges are golden, 15 to 16 minutes, rotating cookie sheets between upper

and lower oven racks halfway through. Transfer cookies to wire racks; cool 10 minutes.

6 Meanwhile, in small bowl, whisk together remaining 1½ cups sugar and 1½ teaspoons lemon peel with reserved lemon juice until blended. Dip tops of warm cookies into glaze and place on wire racks set over waxed paper to catch drips. Allow glaze to set, about 20 minutes.

7 Repeat with remaining dough and glaze, adding a little water to glaze if it begins to thicken.

each cookie About 75 calories, 1g protein, 9g carbohydrate, 4g total fat (3g saturated), 0g fiber, 11mg cholesterol, 65mg sodium

sugar cookies

Sugar cookies are the ideal holiday cookie—they can be frosted and dressed up in countless ways to suit any occasion.

active time 45 minutes plus chilling and decorating   **bake time** 10 minutes per batch   **makes** about 96 (3-inch) cookies

1 cup butter (2 sticks), softened (no substitutions)

½ cup sugar

1 large egg

1 tablespoon vanilla extract

3 cups all-purpose flour

½ teaspoon baking powder

Ornamental Frosting (opposite, optional)

Colored sugar crystals, edible glitter, sprinkles, small round candies, and/or gumdrops (optional)

each cookie without frosting About 40 calories, 1g protein, 5g carbohydrate, 2g total fat (1g saturated), 0g fiber, 7mg cholesterol, 20mg sodium

1 Preheat oven to 350°F. In large bowl, with mixer on low speed, beat butter and sugar until blended. On high, beat until light and creamy. On low speed, beat in egg and vanilla. Beat in flour and baking powder just until blended.

2 Divide dough into 4 equal pieces. Flatten each into a disk; wrap and refrigerate until dough is firm, 1 hour. (Or freeze 30 minutes.)

3 On lightly floured surface, with floured rolling pin, roll 1 piece dough ½ inch thick. With floured cookie cutters, cut out as many cookies as possible; wrap and refrigerate trimmings. Place cookies, 1 inch apart, on two ungreased large cookie sheets.

4 Bake until lightly browned, 10 to 12 minutes, rotating cookie sheets between upper and lower oven racks halfway through. Transfer cookies to wire racks to cool. Repeat with remaining dough and trimmings.

5 When cookies are cool, if desired, prepare Ornamental Frosting and decorate cookies. While frosting is still wet, sprinkle with sugar crystals, glitter, or sprinkles, or press on candies, if you like. Allow frosting to dry completely, about 1 hour.

ornamental frosting

This fluffy frosting is perfect for decorating sugar cookies. The recipe originally called for three raw egg whites, and you can use them if pasteurized eggs are sold in your area. We prefer meringue powder, which is available at many supermarkets and baking supply stores.

active time 10 minutes plus decorating
makes about 3 cups

1 In bowl, with mixer on medium speed, beat confectioners' sugar, meringue powder, and ⅓ cup water until mixture is blended and so stiff that knife drawn through it leaves a clean-cut path, about 5 minutes.

2 Tint frosting with food colorings if desired; keep covered with plastic wrap to prevent drying out. With small spatula, paintbrushes, or writing tips attached to decorating bags, apply frosting to cookies. (You may need to thin frosting with a little warm water to obtain the right spreading or piping consistency.)

1 package (16 ounces) confectioners' sugar

3 tablespoons meringue powder (see note above)

⅓ cup warm water, plus more if needed

Assorted food colorings (optional)

each tablespoon About 40 calories, 0g protein, 10g carbohydrate, 0g total fat (0g saturated), 0g fiber, 0mg cholesterol, 2mg sodium

pistachio and cherry biscotti

These fruit-and-nut biscotti are so pretty, you may want to pack them in cellophane bags for holiday gifts.

active time 45 minutes plus cooling   **bake time** 40 minutes per batch
makes 72 biscotti

2 cups all-purpose flour

1 cup sugar

1 teaspoon baking powder

¼ teaspoon salt

⅛ teaspoon ground cinnamon

4 tablespoons cold butter or margarine, cut into pieces

3 large eggs, lightly beaten

1 cup dried tart cherries

1 cup shelled pistachios (4 ounces), toasted (page 11) and coarsely chopped

1 teaspoon vanilla extract

1 Preheat oven to 350°F.

2 In large bowl, whisk flour, sugar, baking powder, salt, and cinnamon until blended. With pastry blender or two knives used scissor-fashion, cut in butter until mixture resembles fine crumbs.

3 Spoon ½ tablespoon beaten egg into cup and reserve. Add cherries, pistachios, vanilla, and remaining beaten eggs to flour mixture; stir until evenly moistened. Press dough together to form a ball.

4 Divide dough into quarters. On each of two large ungreased cookie sheets, shape 2 pieces dough into 9" by 2" logs placed 4 inches apart. Use pastry brush to coat tops and sides of logs with reserved egg.

5 Bake logs 25 minutes, rotating cookie sheets between upper and lower racks halfway through. Place sheets on wire racks to cool 10 minutes.

6 On cutting board, using a serrated knife, cut each warm log crosswise on diagonal into ½-inch-thick slices. Place slices upright, ¼ inch apart, on cookie sheets; bake 15 minutes. Set sheets on wire racks until biscotti cool completely.

each biscotto About 110 calories, 2g protein, 16g carbohydrate, 5g total fat (2g saturated), 20mg cholesterol, 45mg sodium

chocolate almond meringues

These dainty meringues are dipped first in bittersweet chocolate, then in roasted almonds. Heavenly! For photo, see page 22.

active time 40 minutes plus cooling **bake time** 1 hour 30 minutes
makes about 54 cookies

3 large egg whites

¼ teaspoon almond extract

⅛ teaspoon cream of tartar

pinch salt

½ cup sugar

¾ cup roasted salted almonds, finely chopped

5 squares (5 ounces) bittersweet chocolate, chopped

each cookie About 35 calories, 1g protein, 4g carbohydrate, 2g total fat (1g saturated), 0g fiber, 0mg cholesterol, 10mg sodium

1 Preheat oven to 200°F. Line two cookie sheets with parchment.
2 In medium bowl, with mixer on high speed, beat egg whites, almond extract, cream of tartar, and salt until soft peaks form. With mixer running, sprinkle in sugar, 2 tablespoons at a time, beating until sugar dissolves and meringue stands in stiff, glossy peaks when beaters are lifted.
3 Spoon meringue into decorating bag fitted with ¾-inch round tip, or into large zip-tight plastic bag with small hole cut in one corner. Pipe meringue into 1-inch rounds, 1 inch apart, onto parchment.
4 Bake until crisp, 1 hour 30 minutes to 1 hour 40 minutes, rotating cookie sheets between upper and lower oven racks halfway through.
5 Cool meringues on cookie sheets on wire racks.
6 Meanwhile, place nuts on plate. In small glass bowl, microwave chocolate on Medium 1 minute 30 seconds or until melted, stirring every 30 seconds.
7 Line cookie sheet with parchment. Dip bottom third of each meringue in chocolate, then nuts and place on prepared pans; let stand 1 hour to set.

chocolate hazelnut macaroons

Chocolate and hazelnut is a delectable flavor combination. Although these chewy-crisp cookies are delicious on their own, you can make them outright decadent by sandwiching two together with some melted chocolate.

active time 30 minutes   **bake time** 10 minutes per batch
makes about 30 cookies

1 Preheat oven to 350°F. Toast and skin hazelnuts (page 11). Line two large cookie sheets with foil, do not grease foil.

2 In food processor with knife blade attached, process hazelnuts, sugar, cocoa, chocolate, and salt until nuts and chocolate are finely ground. Add egg whites and vanilla; process until blended.

3 Drop dough by rounded teaspoons, 2 inches apart, onto prepared cookie sheets. Bake until tops feel firm when pressed lightly, 10 minutes, rotating cookie sheets between upper and lower oven racks halfway through. Cool on cookie sheets on wire racks. Repeat with remaining dough.

1 cup hazelnuts (4 ounces)

1 cup sugar

¼ cup unsweetened cocoa

1 square (1 ounce) unsweetened chocolate, chopped

⅛ teaspoon salt

2 large egg whites

1 teaspoon vanilla extract

each cookie About 50 calories, 1g protein, 7g carbohydrate, 3g total fat (1g saturated), 1g fiber, 0mg cholesterol, 10mg sodium

hermit bars

Originating in New England in clipper-ship days, these spicy fruit bars got their name because they keep so well. Sailors stowed them away "like hermits" for snacking on long voyages.

active time 20 minutes plus cooling   **bake time** 13 minutes per batch
makes 32 bars

2 cups all-purpose flour

1 teaspoon ground cinnamon

½ teaspoon baking powder

½ teaspoon baking soda

½ teaspoon ground ginger

¼ teaspoon ground nutmeg

¼ teaspoon salt

⅛ teaspoon ground cloves

1 cup packed brown sugar

½ cup butter or margarine (1 stick), softened

⅓ cup dark molasses

1 large egg

1 cup dark seedless raisins

1 cup pecans (4 ounces), toasted and coarsely chopped (optional)

each bar About 105 calories, 1g protein, 19g carbohydrate, 3g total fat (2g saturated), 0g fiber, 15mg cholesterol, 80mg sodium

1 Preheat oven to 350°F. Grease and flour two large cookie sheets.

2 In large bowl, with wire whisk, mix flour, cinnamon, baking powder, baking soda, ginger, nutmeg, salt, and cloves.

3 In separate large bowl, with mixer on medium speed, beat brown sugar and butter until light and fluffy. Beat in molasses until well combined. Beat in egg. With mixer on low speed, beat in flour mixture just until blended, occasionally scraping bowl with rubber spatula. With spoon, stir in raisins and pecans, if using, just until combined.

4 Divide dough into quarters. With lightly floured hands, shape each quarter into 12" by 1½" log. On each prepared cookie sheet, place 2 logs, leaving about 3 inches in between.

5 Bake until logs flatten and edges are firm, 13 to 15 minutes, rotating cookie sheets between upper and lower oven racks halfway through. Place sheets on wire racks to cool 15 minutes.

6 Transfer logs to cutting board. Slice each log crosswise into 8 bars. Transfer to wire racks to cool completely.

lemon bars

You can make these ahead—cover and freeze the bars when cool, but don't dust them with sugar until they're thawed. For photo, see page 6.

active time 25 minutes   **bake time** 40 minutes   **makes** 32 bars

¾ cup butter (1½ sticks), softened (do not use margarine)

2¼ cups all-purpose flour

⅔ cup plus 1 tablespoon confectioners' sugar

3 to 4 large lemons

6 large eggs

2 cups granulated sugar

1 teaspoon baking powder

¾ teaspoon salt

each bar: About 145 calories, 2g protein, 22g carbohydrate, 6g total fat (3g saturated), 52mg cholesterol, 126mg sodium

1 Preheat oven to 350°F. Line 13" by 9" baking pan with foil (see opposite); grease foil.

2 In food processor with knife blade attached, pulse butter, 2 cups flour, and ⅔ cup confectioners' sugar until mixture is moist but crumbly. Dough should hold together when pressed between two fingers. Sprinkle mixture evenly into prepared pan. Bake until lightly browned, 20 to 25 minutes.

3 Meanwhile, prepare filling: From lemons, grate 2½ teaspoons peel and squeeze ⅔ cup juice. In large bowl, with wire whisk, beat eggs. Add lemon peel and juice, granulated sugar, baking powder, salt, and remaining ¼ cup flour; whisk until well blended

4 Whisk filling again and pour over hot crust. Bake bars until filling is just set and golden around edges, 18 to 22 minutes. Transfer pan to wire rack. Sift remaining 1 tablespoon confectioners' sugar over warm filling. Cool bars completely in pan on wire rack.

5 When cool, lift foil and transfer pastry to cutting board; peel foil from sides. If you like, trim edges of pastry. Cut lengthwise into 4 strips, then cut each strip crosswise into 8 pieces.

LINING A PAN WITH FOIL

To easily remove bars from a pan after baking, line the pan:

STEP 1 Turn pan bottom side up. Cover surface tightly with foil, shiny side out. Remove foil.

STEP 2 Turn pan right side up and fit molded foil into it, smoothing foil to fit into edges.

cocoa brownies

Whip up these easy saucepan brownies on the spur of the moment with pantry staples.

active time 10 minutes   bake time 25 minutes   makes 16 brownies

½ cup all-purpose flour

½ cup unsweetened cocoa

¼ teaspoon baking powder

¼ teaspoon salt

½ cup butter or margarine (1 stick)

1 cup sugar

2 large eggs

1 teaspoon vanilla extract

1 cup walnuts, coarsely chopped (optional)

each brownie About 130 calories, 2g protein, 17g carbohydrate, 7g total fat (4g saturated), 1g fiber, 42mg cholesterol, 110mg sodium

1 Preheat oven to 350°F. Line 9-inch square baking pan with foil (see page 45); grease foil. In small bowl, with wire whisk, mix flour, cocoa, baking powder, and salt.

2 In 3-quart saucepan, melt butter over low heat. Remove from heat and stir in sugar. Stir in eggs, one at a time, until well blended; add vanilla. Stir flour mixture into sugar mixture until blended. Stir in nuts. Spread batter evenly in prepared pan.

3 Bake until toothpick inserted 2 inches from center comes out almost clean, about 25 minutes. Cool completely in pan on wire rack.

4 When cool, lift foil, with brownie, out of pan; peel foil away from sides. Cut into 4 strips, then cut each strip crosswise into 4 pieces.

german chocolate brownies

These brownies boast a chocolate base made with sweetened baking chocolate and a caramel and coconut-pecan frosting, just like their namesake layer cake. But the beauty of these easy bars is you can whip up the batter in a single pan and the frosting in one bowl.

active time 25 minutes   **bake time** 45 minutes   **makes** 36 brownies

1 Preheat oven to 350°F. Line 13" by 9" baking pan with foil (see page 45); grease foil.

2 Prepare brownie: In 3-quart saucepan, heat butter and chocolate over medium-low heat until melted, stirring frequently. Remove saucepan from heat; stir in 1 cup brown sugar. Add eggs and 1 teaspoon vanilla; stir until well mixed. Stir in flour and ½ teaspoon salt just until blended. Spread batter evenly in prepared pan.

3 Prepare topping: In medium bowl, with wire whisk, beat egg whites until foamy. Stir in coconut, pecans, remaining ½ cup brown sugar, ½ teaspoon vanilla, ⅛ teaspoon salt, milk, and almond extract until well combined. Spread topping over batter.

4 Bake until toothpick inserted 2 inches from edge comes out almost clean and topping turns golden brown, 45 to 50 minutes. Cool completely in pan on wire rack.

5 When cool, lift foil, with brownie, out of pan; peel foil away from sides. Cut lengthwise into 6 strips, then cut each strip crosswise into 6 pieces.

½ cup butter or margarine (1 stick)

2 packages (4 ounces each) sweet baking chocolate, chopped

1½ cups packed brown sugar

3 large eggs, lightly beaten

1½ teaspoons vanilla extract

1 cup all-purpose flour

⅝ teaspoons salt

3 large egg whites

2 cups sweetened flaked coconut

1 cup pecans, toasted (see page 11) and chopped

¼ cup whole milk

⅛ teaspoon almond extract

each brownie About 150 calories, 2g protein, 18g carbohydrate, 8g total fat (4g saturated), 1g fiber, 25mg cholesterol, 85mg sodium

hazelnut brownies

Nutella is a chocolate-hazelnut spread that was created in Italy in the 1940s by Pietro Ferrero. At that time, chocolate was in short supply due to the war, so he stretched what he had by adding ground hazelnuts. Today this spread can be found in supermarkets, usually near the peanut butter.

active time 30 minutes **bake time** 25 minutes
makes 24 brownies

1 Preheat oven to 350°F. Line 13" by 9" baking pan with foil (see page 45); grease foil. In small bowl, with wire whisk, mix flour and salt.

2 In 3-quart saucepan, melt butter and chocolates over low heat, stirring frequently, until smooth. Remove from heat; stir in Nutella. Add sugar and vanilla; stir until well blended. Add eggs; stir well. Stir in flour mixture and nuts, just until blended. Spread batter evenly in prepared pan.

3 Bake until toothpick inserted 2 inches from edge comes out almost clean, 25 to 30 minutes. Cool in pan on wire rack.

4 When cool, lift foil, with brownie, out of pan; peel foil away from sides. Cut lengthwise into 4 strips, then cut each strip crosswise into 6 pieces.

1 cup all-purpose flour

½ teaspoon salt

¾ cup butter or margarine (1½ sticks)

4 squares (4 ounces) unsweetened chocolate

2 squares (2 ounces) semisweet chocolate

½ cup Nutella or other chocolate-hazelnut spread (about half 13-ounce jar)

1½ cups sugar

1 teaspoon vanilla extract

4 large eggs, lightly beaten

1 cup hazelnuts (4 ounces), toasted (page 11) and coarsely chopped

each brownie About 230 calories, 4g protein, 23g carbohydrate, 15g total fat (6g saturated), 2g fiber, 52mg cholesterol, 125mg sodium

butterscotch blondies

These classic favorites go from saucepan to baking pan in one easy step. We included pecans, but you can swap in a half cup of chocolate or butterscotch chips, dried fruit, or sweetened flaked coconut, if you like.

active time 15 minutes **bake time** 20 minutes
makes 24 blondies

1 cup all-purpose flour

2 teaspoons baking powder

¾ teaspoon salt

6 tablespoons butter or margarine

1¾ cups packed light brown sugar

2 teaspoons vanilla extract

2 large eggs, lightly beaten

1 cup pecans (4 ounces), coarsely chopped

each blondie About 145 calories, 2g protein, 20g carbohydrate, 7g total fat (2g saturated), 1g fiber, 26mg cholesterol, 150mg sodium

1 Preheat oven to 350°F. Line 13" by 9" baking pan with foil (see page 45); grease foil. On waxed paper, combine flour, baking powder, and salt.

2 In 3-quart saucepan, melt butter over medium heat. Remove from heat; stir in brown sugar and vanilla. Add eggs; stir until well mixed. Stir in flour mixture and pecans just until blended. Spread batter evenly in prepared pan.

3 Bake until toothpick inserted 2 inches from edge comes out almost clean, 20 to 25 minutes. Do not overbake; blondie will firm as it cools. Cool completely in pan on wire rack.

4 When cool, lift foil, with blondie, out of pan; peel foil away from sides. Cut lengthwise into 4 strips, then cut each strip crosswise into 6 pieces.

brown sugar and pecan fingers

This shortbread-style dough is rolled directly onto the cookie sheet, then cut into fingers after baking. For photo, see page 2.

active time 25 minutes   **bake time** 20 minutes
makes 24 bars

1 Preheat oven to 350°F. In large bowl, with mixer on medium speed, beat butter, sugars, vanilla, and salt until creamy, about 2 minutes. On low speed, gradually beat in flour until just evenly moistened. With hand, press dough together to form ball.

2 Divide dough in half. On one side of ungreased large cookie sheet, roll half of dough, covered with waxed paper, lengthwise into 12" by 5" rectangle. Repeat with remaining dough on other side of sheet, leaving 1½ inches between rectangles. With fork, prick dough at 1-inch intervals. Press tines of fork along long sides of rectangles to form decorative edge. Sprinkle pecans evenly over rectangles; press gently to make nuts adhere.

3 Bake until edges are lightly browned, 20 to 25 minutes. While pastry is still warm, cut each rectangle crosswise into 12 thin bars. Transfer to wire racks to cool.

¾ cup butter or margarine (1½ sticks), softened

⅓ cup packed dark brown sugar

¼ cup granulated sugar

1 teaspoon vanilla extract

¼ teaspoon salt

1¾ cups all-purpose flour

½ cup pecans, chopped

each bar About 120 calories, 1g protein, 12g carbohydrate, 8g total fat (4g saturated), 0g fiber, 16mg cholesterol, 90mg sodium

whoopie pies

You'll love these soft, marshmallow-filled chocolate sandwiches.

active time 30 minutes plus cooling bake time 12 minutes
makes 12 whoopie pies

COOKIES

2 cups all-purpose flour

1 cup granulated sugar

½ cup unsweetened cocoa

1 teaspoon baking soda

6 tablespoons butter or margarine, melted

¾ cup milk

1 large egg

1 teaspoon vanilla extract

¼ teaspoon salt

MARSHMALLOW-CREME FILLING

6 tablespoons butter or margarine, slightly softened

1 cup confectioners' sugar

1 jar (7 to 7½ ounces) marshmallow creme

1 teaspoon vanilla extract

each whoopie pie About 365 calories, 4g protein, 59g carbohydrate, 14g total fat (8g saturated), 1g fiber, 51mg cholesterol, 290mg sodium

1 Preheat oven to 350°F. Grease two large cookie sheets.

2 Prepare cookies: In large bowl, combine flour, sugar, cocoa, and baking soda. Stir in melted butter, milk, egg, vanilla, and salt until smooth.

3 Drop dough by heaping tablespoons, 2 inches apart, onto prepared cookie sheets, placing 12 rounds on each sheet. Bake until cookies are puffy and toothpick inserted in center comes out clean, 12 to 14 minutes, rotating sheets between upper and lower racks halfway through. With spatula, transfer cookies to wire racks to cool completely.

4 When cookies are cool, prepare marshmallow-creme filling: In large bowl, with mixer on medium speed, beat butter until smooth. Reduce speed to low; gradually beat in confectioners' sugar. Beat in marshmallow creme and vanilla until smooth.

5 Spread 1 rounded tablespoon filling on flat side of 12 cookies. Top with remaining cookies.

Strawberry Cream Cake (recipe page 60)

cakes & cupcakes

PERFECT CAKES, EVERY TIME

Boxed cake mixes and canned frosting win points for convenience, and they do have their ingenious uses (see Ice Cream Cone Cupcakes, page 76). But once you taste deluxe originals like our Vanilla Chiffon Cake and Lemon Ricotta Cheesecake, there's no turning back. You don't need to be an experienced baker to whip up a great cake, but knowing the basics helps. Follow these tips to create your own sweet sensations at home.

* To dust pan with flour (or cocoa, for chocolate cakes), sprinkle about 1 tablespoon into a greased pan, rotate and tap the pan to disperse it evenly, then discard the excess. For cupcake pans, we like paper or foil liners—they produce moister cakes with rounder tops than if you grease each metal cup.

* Position your oven racks so the cake is in the center of the oven. If you're baking two layers, stagger the pans on one rack if they'll fit, keeping them at least an inch from the sides of the oven and making sure they don't touch each other, so heat can circulate. Rotate them about two-thirds of the way through the baking time.

* After the minimum baking time, touch the center of the cake lightly with your fingertip. If no imprint remains, the cake is done. Alternatively, insert a wooden toothpick in the center of the cake and see if it comes out clean.

* Allow the cake to cool in the pan for 10 to 15 minutes on a wire rack. (If you leave it in the pan too long, it will steam and get soggy.) Then run a knife around the edge and invert the cake onto the rack to finish cooling, about 2 hours for thick loaves and fluted shapes.

* If a cake does stick to the pan, it might help to put it back in the oven at the original baking temperature for a few minutes.

* When the cake is completely cooled, it's ready to be frosted—or wrapped, if you're not decorating it pronto. If you plan to ice it the next day, wrap it tightly in plastic and then aluminum foil; keep it

FROSTING LAYER CAKES

It is easiest to frost a cake if it is elevated and can be turned. If you don't own a cake-decorating stand, consider placing your cake on a serving plate set on a large coffee can to make it easy to rotate.

Brush off any crumbs and use a serrated knife to trim away crisp edges. Place the first layer, rounded side down, on the serving plate. To keep the plate clean, tuck strips of waxed paper under the cake, covering the plate edge. Using a narrow metal spatula, spread ½ to ⅔ cup frosting on the layer top, spreading it almost to the edge. Top with the second cake layer, rounded side up. Thinly frost the cake by first coating the top of the cake, then the side—this layer will hold any crumbs firmly in place.

Finish with a thicker layer of frosting. Smooth the edge where the top and side of the frosting meet by sweeping and swirling the frosting toward the center of the cake. Slip out the waxed paper strips and discard them.

at room temperature. If you don't plan to ice it for several days, freeze it. Then let the frozen cake stand at room temperature, fully wrapped, until thawed.

chocolate cake

Try this for devilishly good layers. It pairs perfectly with Chocolate Buttercream (page 83). See "Frosting Layer Cakes" on page 57 for tips on assembling and icing.

active time 20 minutes **bake time** 30 to 50 minutes, depending on pan
makes 16 servings

2 cups all-purpose flour

1 cup unsweetened cocoa

2 teaspoons baking powder

1 teaspoon baking soda

½ teaspoon salt

1⅓ cups buttermilk

2 teaspoons vanilla extract

1 cup butter or margarine (2 sticks), softened

2 cups sugar

4 large eggs

each serving unfrosted cake About 295 calories, 5g protein, 41g carbohydrate, 14g total fat (3g saturated), 1g fiber, 54mg cholesterol, 385mg sodium

1 Preheat oven to 350°F. Grease three 8-inch round or two 9-inch round cake pans, or one 13" by 9" baking pan. Line each pan with waxed paper; grease paper and dust with flour.

2 On separate sheet of waxed paper, combine flour, cocoa, baking powder, baking soda, and salt. In 2-cup measuring cup, mix buttermilk and vanilla. Set aside.

3 In large bowl, with mixer on low speed, beat butter and sugar until blended. Increase speed to high; beat until creamy, about 2 minutes. Reduce speed to medium-low; add eggs, one at a time, beating well after each.

4 With mixer on low speed, alternately add flour mixture and buttermilk mixture, beginning and ending with flour mixture; beat just until batter is smooth, occasionally scraping bowl with spatula.

5 Pour batter into pans. Bake until toothpick inserted in center of cake comes out with a few crumbs attached, 30 to 35 minutes for round layers or 45 to 50 minutes for sheet cake. Cool in pans on wire racks 10 minutes. With small knife, loosen layer cakes from sides of pans and invert onto wire racks; remove waxed paper and cool cakes completely.

strawberry cream cake

This three-tier stunner, alternating peak-season berries with light and spongy cake, only looks decadent. A cinch to prepare (and less caloric than layer cake), the batter subs tangy low-fat buttermilk for whole milk, and the filling's cream is lightened with yogurt. For photo, see page 54.

active time 50 minutes plus cooling **bake time** 18 minutes
makes 12 servings

2 cups nonfat plain yogurt

2 cups all-purpose flour

½ cup whole wheat flour

1½ teaspoons baking powder

½ teaspoons baking soda

½ teaspoons salt

1 lemon

1 cup low-fat buttermilk

¼ cup canola oil

1½ teaspoons vanilla extract

1½ cups plus 3 tablespoons granulated sugar

2 large eggs

2 large egg whites

2 pounds strawberries

½ cup heavy or whipping cream

⅓ cup plus 1 tablespoon confectioners' sugar

6 tablespoons reduced-sugar strawberry preserves

1 In medium sieve set over deep medium bowl, place basket-style coffee filter or paper towel. Spoon yogurt into filter; cover and refrigerate 2 hours to drain.

2 Preheat oven to 350°F; set one rack in upper third of oven and one rack in lower third. Spray three 9-inch round cake pans with nonstick cooking spray with flour. (Or grease pans, line bottoms with parchment paper, grease paper, and dust with flour.)

3 On waxed paper, combine flours, baking powder and soda, and salt; set aside. From lemon, grate 1 tablespoon peel and squeeze 2 tablespoons juice. In small bowl, whisk together buttermilk, canola oil, lemon peel and juice, and 1 teaspoon vanilla until blended.

4 In large bowl, with mixer on low speed, beat 1½ cups granulated sugar with eggs and egg whites until blended. Increase speed to high; beat 5 minutes, or until mixture is pale and thickened, scraping bowl with rubber spatula. With spatula, fold in flour mixture, alternating with buttermilk

mixture, just until blended, beginning and ending with flour.

5 Spoon batter evenly into prepared pans. Stagger pans on racks, placing two on upper rack and one on lower rack so that upper pans are not directly above lower one. Bake 18 to 20 minutes, or until toothpick inserted in center comes out clean. Cool in pans on wire racks 10 minutes. With small knife, loosen cakes from sides of pans; invert onto racks. Cool completely, about 30 minutes.

6 Meanwhile, reserve 8 small whole strawberries for garnish. Hull remaining strawberries and cut each in half. In large bowl, mix hulled strawberries with remaining 3 tablespoons granulated sugar and let stand 10 minutes.

7 Meanwhile, in medium bowl, with mixer on high speed, beat cream until stiff peaks form. Beat in ⅓ cup confectioners' sugar and remaining ½ teaspoon vanilla until blended. Fold in drained yogurt. Set aside ½ cup filling for top of cake. Place 1 cake layer, rounded side down, on plate.

8 Spread cake layer with 3 tablespoons strawberry preserves. Top with half of remaining filling, spreading to 1 inch from edge of layer. Arrange half of strawberries, with some of their juices, evenly over filling.

9 Lightly press second cake layer on top and repeat step 8 with remaining preserves, filling, and strawberries. Top with third cake layer. Sift remaining 1 tablespoon confectioners' sugar evenly over cake. Spoon reserved ½ cup filling onto center of cake and garnish with reserved strawberries. Serve immediately.

each serving About 355 calories, 8g protein, 60g carbohydrate, 10g total fat (6g saturated), 3g fiber, 51mg cholesterol, 275mg sodium

vanilla chiffon cake

This tall, handsome cake doesn't need icing, just a dusting of confectioners' sugar and some fresh berries served on the side.

active time 20 minutes **bake time** 1 hour 15 minutes
makes 16 servings

1 Preheat oven to 325°F. In large bowl, combine flour, 1 cup granulated sugar, baking powder, and salt. Make a well in center. Add water, oil, egg yolks, and vanilla; with wire whisk, stir until smooth.

2 In separate large bowl, with mixer on high speed, beat all egg whites and cream of tartar until soft peaks form. Sprinkle in remaining ½ cup granulated sugar, 2 tablespoons at a time, beating until sugar has dissolved and egg whites stand in stiff, glossy peaks when beaters are lifted. With rubber spatula, gently fold one-third of beaten egg whites into egg yolk mixture, then fold in remaining egg whites until blended.

3 Scrape batter into ungreased 9- or 10-inch tube pan; spread evenly. Bake until cake springs back when lightly pressed with finger, about 1 hour 15 minutes. Invert cake in pan onto large metal funnel or bottle; cool completely. Run thin knife around cake to loosen from side and center tube of pan; lift tube to separate cake from pan side. Invert cake onto plate and remove tube. Dust with confectioners' sugar.

2¼ cups cake flour (not self-rising)

1½ cups granulated sugar

1 tablespoon baking powder

1 teaspoon salt

¾ cup cold water

½ cup vegetable oil

5 large eggs, separated

1 tablespoon vanilla extract

2 large egg whites

½ teaspoon cream of tartar

Confectioners' sugar

each serving About 215 calories, 4g protein, 3g carbohydrate, 9g total fat (1g saturated), 66mg cholesterol, 265mg sodium

chocolate pudding cake

Rich chocolate cake, creamy chocolate pudding served warm. What more could any chocolate lover hope for?

active time 10 minutes bake time 30 minutes makes 6 servings

1 cup all-purpose baking mix with buttermilk

⅓ cup granulated sugar

¾ cup unsweetened cocoa

¼ cup packed brown sugar

4 tablespoons butter or margarine

½ cup whole milk

1 teaspoon vanilla extract

1 cup heavy or whipping cream (optional)

each serving About 265 calories, 4g protein, 39g carbohydrate, 13g total fat (7g saturated), 4g fiber, 23mg cholesterol, 360 mg sodium

1 Preheat oven to 350°F. In 1-quart saucepan, heat 1¾ cups water to boiling over high heat.

2 In medium bowl, combine baking mix, granulated sugar, and ½ cup cocoa. In small bowl, combine brown sugar and remaining ¼ cup cocoa.

3 In small microwave-safe bowl, heat butter in microwave on High 45 seconds or just until butter melts, stirring once. Stir butter, milk, and vanilla into baking mix mixture until blended. Pour batter into ungreased 8-inch square baking dish. Sprinkle evenly with brown-sugar mixture. Pour boiling water evenly over mixture in baking dish.

4 Bake 30 minutes (batter will separate into cake and pudding layers). Cool on wire rack 5 minutes. If you like, in medium bowl, with mixer on medium speed, beat cream until stiff peaks form. Serve cake warm topped with whipped cream.

warm chocolate soufflé cakes

These rich, chocolate delights are baked in individual ramekins to ensure an elegant presentation. Top them off with a dollop of whipped cream, if you like.

active time 30 minutes plus cooling bake time 40 minutes
makes 10 servings

1 Preheat oven to 350°F. In 4-quart saucepan, melt butter, chocolate, and sugar over low heat. Cool.

2 Grease ten 6-ounce ramekins and dust with flour.

3 In small bowl, with mixer on high speed, beat egg yolks until thick, about 3 minutes. In large bowl, with mixer on high speed, beat egg whites until stiff peaks form. Whisk yolks into chocolate mixture; fold in whites and flour.

4 Place ramekins in roasting pan. Spoon batter into ramekins. Carefully pour boiling water into pan to come halfway up sides of ramekin. Bake until knife inserted near edge comes out clean, 40 minutes. Invert to serve.

¾ cup butter (1½ sticks), cut up (no substitutions)

8 squares (8 ounces) semisweet chocolate, chopped

1 cup sugar

6 large eggs, separated

2 tablespoons all-purpose flour, sifted

each serving About 365 calories, 6g protein, 34g carbohydrate, 25g total fat (14g saturated), 2g fiber, 167mg cholesterol, 185mg sodium

rum raisin applesauce cake

Dark Jamaican rum gives this spiced Bundt cake its rich flavor.

active time 30 minutes plus cooling and setting   bake time 50 minutes
makes 16 servings

1 Preheat oven to 350°F. Grease 10-cup fluted baking pan or 9-inch tube pan; dust with flour.
2 On waxed paper, combine flour, cinnamon, baking soda, salt, and allspice; set aside.
3 In large bowl, with mixer on low speed, beat butter with sugars until blended, frequently scraping bowl with rubber spatula. Increase speed to medium-high; beat until creamy, about 3 minutes, occasionally scraping bowl.
4 Reduce speed to low; add eggs one at a time, beating well after each. Beat in rum and vanilla. Alternately add flour mixture and applesauce, beginning and ending with flour. Stir in raisins.
5 Spread batter evenly into prepared pan. Bake until toothpick inserted in center of cake comes out clean, 50 to 55 minutes.
6 Cool cake in pan on wire rack 15 minutes. With small metal spatula, loosen cake from pan. Invert cake onto plate, then transfer cake right side up to wire rack to cool completely. Drizzle cooled cake with Brown Sugar Rum Glaze; let glaze set at least 20 minutes before serving.

2¼ cups all-purpose flour

1½ teaspoons ground cinnamon

1 teaspoon baking soda

½ teaspoon salt

¼ teaspoon ground allspice

½ cup butter or margarine (1 stick), softened

¾ cup packed brown sugar

½ cup granulated sugar

2 large eggs

⅓ cup dark Jamaican rum

2 teaspoons vanilla extract

1¼ cups sweetened applesauce

1 cup dark seedless raisins

Brown Sugar Rum Glaze (page 85)

each serving About 280 calories, 3g protein, 47g carbohydrate, 9g total fat (6g saturated), 1g fiber, 49mg cholesterol, 250mg sodium

brown sugar pound cake

Dark brown sugar gives this country cake a delicious butterscotch flavor.

active time 30 minutes bake time 50 minutes
makes 16 servings

2 cups all-purpose flour

¾ teaspoon salt

½ teaspoon baking powder

½ teaspoon baking soda

10 tablespoons butter or margarine, softened

1 cup packed dark brown sugar

⅓ cup granulated sugar

2 large eggs

1 tablespoon vanilla extract

¾ cup whole milk

each serving About 210 calories, 3g protein, 30g carbohydrate, 9g total fat (5g saturated), 0g fiber, 49mg cholesterol, 255mg sodium

1 Preheat oven to 325°F. Grease 10-cup fluted baking pan or decorative 9- to 10-cup metal loaf pan; dust pan with flour.

2 On waxed paper, combine flour, salt, baking powder, and baking soda; set aside.

3 In large bowl, with mixer on low speed, beat butter and sugars until blended, frequently scraping bowl with rubber spatula. Increase speed to medium-high; beat until creamy, about 3 minutes, occasionally scraping bowl.

4 Reduce speed to low; add eggs, one at a time, beating well after each. Beat in vanilla. Alternately add flour mixture and milk, beginning and ending with flour; beat just until smooth.

5 Spread batter evenly into prepared pan. Bake until toothpick inserted in center of cake comes out clean, 50 to 60 minutes.

6 Cool cake in pan on wire rack 15 minutes. With small metal spatula, loosen cake from side of pan and invert onto wire rack to cool completely.

raspberry-ribbon coffee cake

Almond paste adds a sweet, mellow flavor and keeps this treat moist for a week.

active time 25 minutes bake time 45 minutes
makes 12 servings

1 Preheat oven to 350°F. Grease and flour 9-inch springform pan.

2 On waxed paper, combine flour, baking powder, and salt.

3 In large bowl, with mixer on low speed, beat almond paste with sugar to sandy consistency. Beat in butter. Increase speed to medium-high; beat until creamy, about 5 minutes, occasionally scraping bowl with rubber spatula.

4 Reduce speed to low; add eggs, one at a time, beating well after each. Beat in vanilla. Alternately add flour mixture and milk, beginning and ending with flour; beat until batter is blended, occasionally scraping bowl.

5 Spread batter evenly into prepared pan. Stir jam until smooth then spoon dollops onto batter. With tip of knife, swirl through jam and batter to create marble design. Sprinkle almonds evenly over top. Bake until toothpick inserted in center of cake comes out clean, 45 to 50 minutes.

6 Cool cake in pan on wire rack 10 minutes. With metal spatula, loosen cake from side of pan. Remove pan side and cool cake on wire rack.

1½ cups all-purpose flour

1½ teaspoons baking powder

¼ teaspoon salt

4 ounces almond paste (about half 7- to 8-ounce tube or can), cut up

¾ cup sugar

6 tablespoons butter or margarine, softened

2 large eggs

1½ teaspoons vanilla extract

½ cup whole milk

⅓ cup seedless red raspberry jam

½ cup sliced natural almonds

each serving About 275 calories, 5g protein, 36g carbohydrate, 12g total fat (5g saturated), 2g fiber, 53mg cholesterol, 180mg sodium

lemon upside-down cake

Sweet brown sugar and tangy lemons combine to make a deliciously different upside-down cake. We added a touch of cornmeal to the batter for a more down-home appeal.

active time 30 minutes **bake time** 45 minutes
makes 12 servings

¾ cup butter or margarine (1½ sticks), softened

1 cup packed light brown sugar

6 lemons

1⅓ cups all-purpose flour

¼ cup yellow cornmeal

2 teaspoons baking powder

½ teaspoon salt

¾ cup granulated sugar

2 large eggs

1 teaspoon vanilla extract

½ cup whole milk

each serving About 315 calories, 4g protein, 46g carbohydrate, 14g total fat (8g saturated), 1g fiber, 70mg cholesterol, 310mg sodium

1 Preheat oven to 350°F. In nonstick 10-inch skillet with oven-safe handle or cast-iron skillet, melt ¼ cup butter with brown sugar over medium heat, stirring often. Cook mixture, stirring until melted, about 2 minutes. Remove from heat.

2 From lemons, grate 2 teaspoons peel. With knife, remove peel and white pith from lemons. Slice lemons into ¼-inch-thick slices; remove seeds. Arrange lemon slices in skillet.

3 On waxed paper, combine flour, cornmeal, baking powder, and salt.

4 In large bowl, with mixer on medium speed, beat remaining ½ cup butter and granulated sugar until creamy. Beat in eggs, one at a time, until well blended. Beat in vanilla and lemon peel.

5 Reduce speed to low. Beat in flour mixture alternately with milk just until blended. Spread batter evenly over lemons.

6 Bake until toothpick inserted in center of cake comes out clean, 45 to 50 minutes. Cool cake in skillet on wire rack 10 minutes, then invert onto plate. Cool 30 minutes to serve warm, or cool completely to serve later.

almond cheesecake

An amaretto crust enhances the almond flavor of this silky-textured cheesecake. If you like, substitute 1 teaspoon almond extract for the almond liqueur called for in the recipe.

. . . .

active time 20 minutes plus cooling and chilling   **bake time** 1 hour 25 minutes
makes 16 servings

. . . .

40 amaretti cookies (about 3 cups)

4 tablespoons butter or margarine, melted

1¼ cups sugar

¼ cup cornstarch

2 packages (8 ounces each) cream cheese, softened

1 container (15 ounces) part-skim ricotta cheese

4 large eggs

1½ cups half-and-half or light cream

¼ cup almond-flavor liqueur

2 teaspoons vanilla extract

1 In food processor, with knife blade attached, blend cookies until fine crumbs form (you should have about 1 cup crumbs).

2 Preheat oven to 375°F. In 9" by 3" springform pan, with fork, stir cookie crumbs and butter until evenly moistened. With hand, press mixture firmly onto bottom of pan. Bake crust 10 minutes. Cool crust completely in pan on wire rack, about 30 minutes. Wrap outside of pan with foil.

3 Turn oven control to 325°F. In small bowl, with wire whisk, mix sugar and cornstarch. In large bowl, with mixer on medium speed, beat cream cheese and ricotta until smooth, about 3 minutes. Reduce speed to low and slowly beat in sugar mixture, then eggs, half-and-half, liqueur, and vanilla just until blended, frequently scraping bowl with rubber spatula (cream-cheese mixture will be very thin).

4 Pour cheese mixture onto crust in pan. Bake until filling is firm 2 inches from edge of pan and center is still jiggly, 1 hour and 15 minutes. Turn off oven; let cheesecake remain in oven 1 hour longer. Remove cheesecake from oven.

Cool completely in pan on wire rack. Cover and refrigerate cheesecake until well chilled, at least 6 hours or overnight. Cheesecake will firm during chilling. (To freeze cheesecake, see "Perfect Presentation," below.)

5 With small metal spatula, gently loosen cake from side of pan. Remove side of pan.

each serving About 325 calories, 8g protein, 29g carbohydrate, 19g total fat (10g saturated), 0g fiber, 101mg cholesterol, 185mg sodium

PERFECT PRESENTATION

Cheesecake taste better a day or so after it's baked, so for exceptional results, make this recipe up to 2 days ahead. If that's not possible, refrigerate for at least 6 hours, as recipe instructs, tightly wrapping the cheesecake with plastic wrap so it does not pick up aromas from other foods in the refrigerator.

This cheesecake also freezes beautifully. After thoroughly chilling, as recipe directs in step 4, remove sides of springform pan from cheesecake and wrap cake tightly in plastic; freeze up to 2 weeks. Unwrap to thaw.

If you want to preslice for easy serving, do it while the cake is still partially frozen. Using a large, sharp knife, cut the cake into 16 slices. Wipe the blade clean after making each cut, then dip the blade in hot water, dry it off quickly, and make the next cut. This will help prevent the gooey cheesecake from sticking to the knife.

new york–style cheesecake

Purists will insist on devouring this cake unadorned, while the more adventurous will enjoy our swirled chocolate variation.

active time 20 minutes plus cooling and chilling　**bake time** 1 hour 5 minutes
makes 16 servings

Simple Crumb Crust, made with graham crackers in a 9-inch springform pan (page 117)

3 packages (8 ounces each) cream cheese, softened

¾ cup sugar

1 tablespoon all-purpose flour

1½ teaspoons vanilla extract

3 large eggs

1 large egg yolk

¼ cup milk

Fresh fruits for garnish (optional)

1　Bake and cool crust as recipe directs. Set oven to 300°F.

2　In large bowl, with mixer on medium speed, beat cream cheese and sugar until smooth and fluffy. Beat in flour and vanilla until well combined.

3　On low speed, beat in eggs and egg yolk, one at a time, beating well after each. Beat in milk just until blended.

4　Pour batter into prepared crust. Bake until filling is set, but 3 inches from center remains slightly wet, and cake is lightly golden, 55 to 60 minutes. Cool completely in pan on wire rack. Refrigerate overnight, then remove side of pan, place cake on plate, and garnish with fruits, if you like.

each serving About 275 calories, 5g protein, 19g carbohydrate, 20g total fat (12g saturated), 0g fiber, 108mg cholesterol, 230mg sodium

chocolate marble cheesecake

Prepare and bake Simple Crumb Crust using **about 27 chocolate wafers** instead of graham crackers. Prepare batter as directed for New York–Style Cheesecake but omit milk. Melt **2 squares**

(2 ounces) semisweet chocolate. In small bowl, stir together **melted chocolate** and **1 cup cheesecake batter**. Pour **remaining plain cheesecake batter** into prepared crust. Spoon **chocolate batter** over top in several dollops. Using knife, swirl chocolate batter through plain batter. Bake, cool, and chill as directed.

each serving About 290 calories, 5g protein, 21g carbohydrate, 21g total fat (12g saturated), 0g fiber, 108mg cholesterol, 220mg sodium

ice cream cone cupcakes

A sweet treat that kids will want to help decorate. These are best eaten the same day they are made, or the cones will become soggy. To ensure that the cakes rise properly and do not overflow, fill each cone no more than two-thirds full.

active time 15 minutes plus cooling and frosting **bake time** 20 minutes
makes 24 cupcakes

1 package (18¼ ounces) yellow or white cake mix

24 waffle-style, flat-bottomed ice cream cones

2 cans (16 ounces each) vanilla and/or chocolate frosting, or 1 recipe Vanilla or Chocolate Buttercream (page 82 or 83)

Assorted sprinkles

each cupcake About 330 calories, 3g protein, 55g carbohydrate, 11g total fat (3g saturated), 1g fiber, 23mg cholesterol, 230mg sodium

1 Preheat oven to 350°F. Prepare cake mix as label directs. Spoon batter into cones, filling each about two-thirds full. Place cones on large cookie sheet or jelly-roll pan for easier handling.

2 Bake cones until toothpick inserted in center of cake comes out clean, 20 to 22 minutes. Cool completely on cookie sheet on wire rack.

3 To decorate cupcakes, with small metal spatula, spread 2 tablespoons frosting on cake in each cone; top with sprinkles.

THE FROSTING ON THE CUPCAKE

Who doesn't love frosting and decorating cupcakes? Here are some helpful tips.

* Use a small metal spatula to spread frosting evenly on cupcakes. If it's too thick to spread, add milk until it reaches the right consistency.

* For piped frosting, spoon our Vanilla or Chocolate Buttercream into a decorating bag fitted with a small decorating tip or other tip you'd like to work with.

* Heavyweight zip-tight plastic bags work well as decorating bags too—especially if you want to work with multiple colored frostings. Simply squeeze frosting to one corner of the bag and snip diagonally to desired size opening.

* Use kitchen shears to cut candy such as shoestring licorice or fruit leather into shapes to top your cupcakes.

* Luster dust, assorted sprinkles, and candy melts are available in stores where cake-decorating supplies are sold. M&M's, peppermints, and many other candies have cupcake-decorating potential too.

golden butter cupcakes

A platter of these classic cupcakes topped with delicious frosting can't be beat. Try them with Chocolate Buttercream (page 83)!

active time 15 minutes plus cooling and frosting **bake time** 20 minutes
makes 24 cupcakes

2 cups all-purpose flour

1½ cups sugar

2½ teaspoons baking powder

1 teaspoon salt

¾ cup butter or margarine (1½ sticks), softened

¾ cup whole milk

1½ teaspoons vanilla extract

3 large eggs

Choice of frosting (pages 82–85)

each unfrosted cupcake
About 155 calories, 2g protein, 21g carbohydrate, 7g total fat (4g saturated), 0g fiber, 44mg cholesterol, 210mg sodium

1 Preheat oven to 350°F. Line twenty-four 2½-inch muffin-pan cups with fluted paper liners.

2 In large bowl, with handheld mixer or heavy-duty mixer fitted with whisk attachment, mix flour, sugar, baking powder, and salt on low speed until combined. Add butter, milk, vanilla, and eggs and beat just until blended. Increase speed to high; beat until creamy, 1 to 2 minutes, occasionally scraping bowl with rubber spatula.

3 Spoon batter into muffin-pan cups. Bake until cupcakes are golden brown and toothpick inserted in center comes out clean, 20 to 25 minutes. Immediately remove cupcakes from pans and cool completely on wire rack.

4 While cupcakes are cooling, prepare frosting; use to decorate cooled cupcakes.

citrus cupcakes

Prepare Golden Butter Cupcakes as directed above, but use only **2 teaspoons baking powder** and add **1 tablespoon freshly grated lemon, lime, or orange peel** with vanilla.

carrot cupcakes

Pair with our Cream Cheese Frosting or your favorite.

active time 25 minutes plus cooling and frosting bake time 25 minutes
makes 24 cupcakes

1 Preheat oven to 350°F. Line twenty-four 2½-inch muffin-pan cups with fluted paper liners. (Do not use foil liners; cupcakes will not bake evenly.)

2 On waxed paper, combine flour, cinnamon, baking powder, baking soda, salt, and nutmeg.

3 In large bowl, with mixer on medium-high speed, beat eggs and sugars until creamy, 2 minutes, frequently scraping bowl with rubber spatula. Beat in pineapple with its juice, oil, and vanilla. Reduce speed to low; gradually add flour mixture and beat just until blended, about 1 minute. Fold in carrots and raisins.

4 Spoon batter into muffin-pan cups. Bake until toothpick inserted in center of cupcake comes out clean, 25 to 30 minutes. Immediately remove from pans and cool completely on wire rack.

5 While cupcakes are cooling, prepare frosting; use to decorate cooled cupcakes.

2¼ cups all-purpose flour

2 teaspoons ground cinnamon

1 teaspoon baking powder

1 teaspoon baking soda

1 teaspoon salt

¼ teaspoon ground nutmeg

2 large eggs

1 cup granulated sugar

½ cup packed brown sugar

1 can (8 ounces) crushed pineapple in juice

½ cup vegetable oil

1 tablespoon vanilla extract

2½ cups lightly packed shredded carrots

⅔ cup dark seedless raisins

Choice of frosting (pages 82–85)

each unfrosted cupcake
About 160 calories, 2g protein, 28g carbohydrate, 5g total fat (0g saturated), 1g fiber, 18mg cholesterol, 180mg sodium

rich chocolate cupcakes

Top these chocolaty cupcakes with a swirl of fudge frosting.
Chocolate lovers will sing your praises.

active time 15 minutes plus cooling and frosting **bake time** 22 minutes
makes 24 cupcakes

1⅓ cups all-purpose flour

⅔ cup unsweetened cocoa

1½ teaspoons baking powder

½ teaspoon baking soda

½ teaspoon salt

1 cup whole milk

1½ teaspoons vanilla extract

1⅓ cups sugar

10 tablespoons butter or margarine, softened

2 large eggs

Choice of frosting (pages 82–85)

each unfrosted cupcake
About 130 calories, 2g protein, 18g carbohydrate, 6g total fat (4g saturated), 1g fiber, 33mg cholesterol, 160mg sodium

1 Preheat oven to 350°F. Line twenty-four 2½-inch muffin-pan cups with fluted paper liners.

2 On waxed paper, combine flour, cocoa, baking powder, baking soda, and salt. In 2-cup liquid measure, mix milk and vanilla; set aside.

3 In large bowl, using handheld mixer or heavy-duty mixer fitted with whisk attachment, beat sugar and butter on low speed, just until blended. Increase speed to high; beat 3 minutes or until mixture is light and creamy. Reduce speed to low; add eggs, one at a time, beating well after each.

4 Add flour mixture alternately with milk mixture, beginning and ending with flour. Beat just until combined, occasionally scraping bowl with rubber spatula.

5 Spoon batter into muffin-pan cups. Bake until toothpick inserted in center of cupcake comes out clean, 22 to 25 minutes. Immediately remove from pans and cool completely on wire rack.

6 While cupcakes are cooling, prepare frosting; use to decorate cooled cupcakes.

vanilla buttercream

This satiny confection is supremely versatile. It's suitable for everything from homey sheet cakes to layer cakes or decorated cupcakes.

active time 20 minutes plus chilling   **makes** 3¼ cups

1 cup sugar

½ cup all-purpose flour

1⅓ cups milk

1 cup butter or margarine (2 sticks), softened

1 tablespoon vanilla extract

each tablespoon About 55 calories, 0g protein, 5g carbohydrate, 4g total fat (1g saturated), 0g fiber, 1mg cholesterol, 50mg sodium

1 In 2-quart saucepan, with wire whisk, mix sugar and flour until combined. Gradually whisk in milk until smooth. Cook over medium-high heat, stirring frequently, until mixture thickens and boils. Reduce heat to low; cook, stirring constantly, 2 minutes. Transfer mixture to bowl. Place plastic wrap directly on surface of mixture; refrigerate and cool completely, 4 hours or overnight. Or, place in freezer 20 to 25 minutes, stirring once.

2 In large bowl, with mixer on medium speed, beat butter until creamy. Gradually beat in cooled milk mixture until blended. Add vanilla and beat until frosting is fluffy.

coloring frosting

For tinting frosting and icings, the pros prefer paste food colors (also called icing colors), which do not dilute the frosting as liquid colors can. Paste colors are extremely intense; add them a tiny bit at a time, using the tip of a toothpick.

chocolate buttercream

This light, creamy frosting should be in every baker's repertoire.

active time 10 minutes makes 2¾ cups

In large bowl, with mixer on low speed, beat confectioners' sugar, butter, milk, vanilla, and chocolate just until mixed. Increase speed to high; beat until light and fluffy, about 2 minutes, frequently scraping bowl with rubber spatula.

2 cups confectioners' sugar

1 cup butter or margarine (2 sticks), softened

3 tablespoons milk

1 teaspoon vanilla extract

6 squares (6 ounces) semisweet chocolate, melted and cooled

each tablespoon About 80 calories, 5g protein, 0g carbohydrate, 6g total fat (3g saturated), 0g fiber, 3mg cholesterol, 51mg sodium

figuring frosting quantities

Here's how much frosting you'll need for the following cake sizes:

8-inch round, two layers	2¼ cups
8-inch round, three layers	2¾ cups
9-inch round, two layers	2⅔ cups
8-inch square, one layer	1⅓ cups
9-inch square, one layer	2 cups
13" by 9", one layer	2⅓ cups
10-inch tube pan	2¼ cups
24 cupcakes	2¼ cups

cream cheese frosting

This creamy frosting is a favorite of many cake lovers. For about one-third less fat, prepare this frosting with light cream cheese, also called Neufchâtel. You'll never miss the extra calories, but the consistency may not be quite as thick. Refrigerate leftover frosting, if any. Bring to room temperature before using.

active time 10 minutes **makes** 1½ cups

1 package (16 ounces) confectioners' sugar (3½ to 4 cups)

1 package cream cheese (8 ounces), softened

4 tablespoons butter or margarine, softened

2 teaspoons vanilla extract

In large bowl, with mixer on low speed, beat confectioners' sugar, cream cheese, butter, and vanilla until blended. Increase speed to medium; beat until frosting is smooth and creamy, about 2 minutes, occasionally scraping bowl with rubber spatula.

each tablespoon About 70 calories, 1g protein, 10g carbohydrate, 3g total fat (2g saturated), 0g fiber, 8mg cholesterol, 35mg sodium

lemony cream-cheese frosting

Prepare Cream Cheese Frosting as directed above, but substitute **1½ teaspoons freshly grated lemon peel** for vanilla.

brown sugar rum glaze

A quick and delicious final touch that tastes great drizzled over our Rum Raisin Applesauce Cake (page 67). It's also yummy on chocolate, spice, or even angel food cake.

active time 8 minutes   **makes** ½ cup

1 In 1-quart measuring cup, heat brown sugar and butter in microwave on High until bubbly, 1 minute and 15 seconds to 1 minute and 45 seconds, stirring twice during cooking. With wire whisk, beat in rum; then whisk in confectioners' sugar until mixture is smooth.

2 Immediately pour glaze over top of cooled cake, letting it run down sides. Allow glaze to set for at least 20 minutes before serving cake.

¼ cup packed light brown sugar

3 tablespoons butter (no substitutions)

1 tablespoon dark Jamaican rum

⅓ cup confectioners' sugar

each ½ tablespoon
About 45 calories, 0g protein, 6g carbohydrate, 2g total fat (1g saturated), 0g fiber, 6mg cholesterol, 25mg sodium

Rustic Apricot Crostata (recipe page 108)

pies & tarts

EASY AS PIE

Intimidated by the thought of making a pie or tart from scratch? Don't be. To ease your way in, try Chocolate Cream and Banana Cream Pies, which feature crumb crusts. Ready to roll? Try classic Lemon Meringue, Pecan, and Blueberry Cream Pies. And then come the tarts—from our lattice-topped Rustic Apricot Crostata to a show-stopping Raspberry Ganache Tart. Here are some pointers to help you along the way.

* Keep both the butter and shortening well chilled; use ice water to mix the ingredients together. A pastry blender is the best utensil, but you can also use two dinner knives, scissor-fashion, to cut in the fat until the mixture resembles coarse crumbs. Using a fork, toss the mixture, sprinkling in ice water, 1 tablespoon at a time, just until the dough is moist enough to come together. If you're using a food processor, process the dough until it just barely comes together (otherwise, you'll end up with a tough crust).

* Dust the work surface and rolling pin lightly with flour and sprinkle a little flour on the dough. To roll dough into a circle, start in the center and roll outward, going right up to—but not over—the edge. Give the dough a quarter turn and repeat the sequence until you have an even circle.

* To transfer a dough round to a pie plate, loosely roll the dough onto the rolling pin, position the pin at one side of the pie plate, and unroll the dough into it. Or, fold the round into quarters, set it in the pie plate, and unfold. Gently ease the dough into the pie plate with your fingertips.

* To prebake (or "blind" bake) the crust before you add the filling, prick the bottom of the crust all over with a fork to keep the crust from blistering as it bakes. Then line it with foil and metal pie weights, dry beans, or uncooked rice.

TWO DECORATIVE BORDERS

FLUTED Using kitchen shears, trim the dough to leave a 1-inch

overhang. Fold this under and pinch it to make a stand-up edge. Push the tip of one index finger against the outside of the rim; with the index finger and thumb of the other hand, press to make a ruffle. Repeat all the way around the pie, leaving about ¼ inch between ruffles.

MINI SHAPES Using kitchen shears, trim the dough edge even with the rim of the pan. Gather the trimmings and roll them ⅛

inch thick. With a tiny cookie cutter or knife, cut out hearts, leaves, or other motifs of equal size. Lightly brush the edge of the piecrust with water, then press the cutouts onto it to encircle the pie.

* Set the pie on a foil-lined cookie sheet and bake it in the lower third of the oven so the bottom crisps and the top doesn't overbrown. If the edges begin browning too fast, cover them loosely with strips of foil or create an aluminum foil circle that covers the outer rim of the crust only.

double fruit pie

Our Double Blueberry Pie recipes has long been a favorite. Only half the fruit is cooked; the other half is stirred in without heating. Choose this old standby or one of three new combinations from the chart.

active time 30 minutes plus cooling and chilling **bake time** 8 minutes
makes 10 servings

VARIATION	BASIC MIX	FRUIT #1	FRUIT #2
DOUBLE BLUEBERRY (GINGERSNAP CRUST, PAGE 117)	½ cup sugar 2 tablespoons cornstarch 2 tablespoons water pinch salt	1½ pints blueberries (about 3¾ cups)	1½ pints blueberries (about 3¾ cups)
APRICOT AND BLACKBERRY (GRAHAM CRACKER CRUST, PAGE 117)	⅔ cup sugar 3 tablespoons cornstarch 1 cup water pinch salt	2 pounds ripe apricots, not peeled, each cut into 8 wedges	½ pint blackberries (about 1½ cups)
MIXED BERRY (VANILLA WAFER CRUST, PAGE 117)	½ cup sugar 3 tablespoons cornstarch 3 tablespoons water pinch salt	1½ pints blueberries (about 3¾ cups)	½ pint strawberries (about 1½ cups), hulled and sliced ½ pint raspberries (about 1½ cups)
PEACH AND RASPBERRY (VANILLA WAFER CRUST, PAGE 117)	½ cup sugar 3 tablespoons cornstarch ¼ cup water pinch salt	2 pounds ripe peaches, peeled, each cut into 8 wedges	1 pint raspberries (about 3 cups)

1. Pick your variation, then prepare Simple Crumb Crust using crumbs suggested in the chart, opposite.
2. Following chart for chosen variation, in 3-quart saucepan, with wire whisk, whisk ingredients for Basic Mix until blended. Add Fruit #1 to sugar mixture; stir to coat evenly.
3. Heat fruit mixture to boiling over medium-high heat, stirring occasionally; boil 2 minutes, stirring constantly. Remove mixture from heat; gently stir in Fruit #2.
4. Spoon filling into cooled crust. Cover and refrigerate until well chilled, about 3 hours.

each serving About 260 calories, 2g protein, 44g carbohydrate, 10g total fat (2g saturated), 4g fiber, 0mg cholesterol, 190mg sodium

chocolate cream pie

Win friends and fans with this indulgent dessert.

active time 35 minutes plus cooling and chilling **bake time** 10 minutes
makes 10 servings

1 Melt 4 tablespoons butter. In 9-inch pie plate, with fork, mix butter, crumbs, and 1 tablespoon sugar until evenly moistened. Press mixture firmly onto bottom and up side of pie plate, making small rim. Bake 10 minutes; cool on wire rack.

2 Meanwhile, in heavy 3-quart saucepan, combine remaining ¾ cup sugar, cornstarch, and salt; with wire whisk, stir in milk until smooth. Cook over medium heat, stirring constantly until mixture has thickened and boils; boil 1 minute longer. In small bowl, lightly beat egg yolks. Beat ½ cup hot milk mixture into beaten egg yolks. Slowly pour egg-yolk mixture back into milk mixture, stirring rapidly to prevent curdling. Cook over low heat, stirring constantly, until mixture is very thick or until temperature on an instant-read thermometer reaches 160°F.

3 Remove from heat and stir in chocolate, remaining 2 tablespoons butter, and vanilla until butter melts and mixture is smooth. Pour hot filling into cooled crust; press plastic wrap directly onto surface. Refrigerate until set, about 4 hours.

4 Just before serving, with mixer on medium speed, beat cream in small bowl until stiff peaks form; spoon over chocolate filling. Top with chocolate curls if desired.

6 tablespoons butter or margarine

1¼ cups chocolate wafer crumbs (24 cookies)

1 tablespoon plus ¾ cup sugar

⅓ cup cornstarch

½ teaspoon salt

3¾ cups whole milk

5 large egg yolks

3 squares (3 ounces) unsweetened chocolate, melted

2 teaspoons vanilla extract

1 cup heavy or whipping cream

Chocolate curls (optional)

each serving About 415 calories, 7g protein, 38g carbohydrate, 28g total fat (16g saturated), 171mg cholesterol, 330mg sodium

strawberry cheesecake pie

A scrumptious "cheesecake" in a fraction of the time.

active time 20 minutes plus cooling and chilling **bake time** 40 minutes

makes 10 servings

Simple Crumb Crust, made with graham crackers (page 117)

12 ounces cream cheese, softened

½ cup sugar

2 large eggs

½ teaspoon vanilla extract

1 pint strawberries

¼ cup red currant jelly

each serving About 320 calories, 5g protein, 31g carbohydrate, 20g total fat (12g saturated), 1g fiber, 96mg cholesterol, 251mg sodium

1 Prepare, bake, and cool crust as recipe directs.

2 Preheat oven to 350°F.

3 In small bowl, with mixer on low speed, beat cream cheese and sugar until smooth, scraping bowl often with rubber spatula. Beat in eggs and vanilla just until blended, scraping bowl often. Pour cheese mixture into cooled crumb crust.

4 Bake until set, about 30 minutes. Cool pie completely on wire rack. Refrigerate pie until ready to serve.

5 Just before serving, hull strawberries and cut each in half lengthwise. Arrange strawberry halves on top of pie. In small saucepan, melt currant jelly over low heat. Spoon melted jelly over strawberries and top of pie.

banana cream pie

Silky vanilla custard, sliced ripe bananas, and a crumb crust made from vanilla wafers form the layers of this heavenly banana cream pie.

active time 30 minutes plus cooling and chilling **bake time** 8 minutes
makes 10 servings

1 Prepare, bake, and cool crust as recipe directs.

2 Meanwhile, in 3-quart saucepan, combine sugar, cornstarch, and salt; stir in milk. Cook over medium heat, stirring constantly, until mixture thickens and boils; boil 1 minute. In small bowl with wire whisk, lightly beat egg yolks; beat in ½ cup hot milk mixture. Slowly pour yolk mixture back into milk, stirring rapidly to prevent curdling. Cook over low heat, stirring constantly, until mixture thickens, about 2 minutes. Remove from heat. Add butter and 1½ teaspoons vanilla; stir until butter melts. Transfer to medium bowl. Lay plastic wrap directly on surface of custard to prevent skin from forming. Refrigerate, stirring occasionally, until cool, about 1 hour.

3 Spoon half of filling into crust. Slice 2 bananas crosswise. Arrange slices on top of filling; spoon remaining filling evenly over bananas. Lay plastic wrap directly on surface of pie; refrigerate 4 hours or up to overnight.

4 Just before serving, in small bowl, with mixer on medium speed, beat cream and remaining ¼ teaspoon vanilla until stiff peaks form when beaters are lifted; spread over pie. Slice remaining banana; arrange around edge.

Simple Crumb Crust, made with vanilla wafers (page 117)

¾ cup sugar

⅓ cup cornstarch

¼ teaspoon salt

3¾ cups milk

5 large egg yolks

2 tablespoons butter or margarine, cut into pieces

1¾ teaspoons vanilla extract

3 ripe medium bananas

¾ cup heavy or whipping cream

each serving About 365 calories, 6g protein, 41g carbohydrate, 21g total fat (12g saturated), 162mg cholesterol, 216mg sodium

lemon meringue pie

Good news for pie lovers: Our luscious no-fail recipe for this all-American classic is a cinch to make.

active time 1 hour 15 minutes plus cooling and chilling   **bake time** 25 minutes

makes 10 servings

Pastry for 9-inch pie (page 118), or frozen deep-dish piecrust, thawed

LEMON FILLING

5 to 6 medium lemons

1 cup sugar

⅓ cup cornstarch

¼ teaspoon salt

1½ cups water

3 large egg yolks

2 tablespoons butter or margarine

MERINGUE TOPPING

4 large egg whites

¼ teaspoon cream of tartar

Pinch salt

½ cup sugar

1 Prepare, bake, and cool pastry crust or deep-dish crust as recipe or label directs.

2 Prepare lemon filling: From lemons, grate 1 tablespoon peel and squeeze ¾ cup juice. In 2-quart saucepan, mix sugar, cornstarch, and salt; stir in water until blended. Cook over medium-high heat, stirring occasionally, until mixture thickens and boils. Boil 1 minute, stirring. Remove from heat.

3 In small bowl, with wire whisk, whisk egg yolks. Stir in ½ cup hot cornstarch mixture until blended; slowly pour yolk mixture back into cornstarch mixture in saucepan, stirring rapidly to prevent curdling. Place saucepan over medium-low heat and cook until mixture comes to a gentle boil, stirring constantly. Cook, stirring, until filling is very thick, 2 to 3 minutes. Remove from heat; stir in butter until melted. Stir in lemon juice and peel; mixture will thin out. Pour into cooled pie shell.

4 Preheat oven to 400°F.

5 Prepare meringue topping: In medium bowl, with mixer on high speed, beat egg whites, cream of tartar, and salt until frothy. Gradually sprinkle in sugar, 2 tablespoons at a time, beating until sugar

completely dissolves and egg whites stand in stiff, glossy peaks when beaters are lifted.

6 Spread meringue over warm filling. To keep meringue from shrinking during baking, make sure it touches edge of crust all around. Use back of wooden spoon to make attractive swirl patterns on top of meringue. Bake until meringue is golden, 6 to 8 minutes. Cool pie completely on wire rack away from draft. Refrigerate at least 1 hour before serving.

each serving About 300 calories, 4g protein, 47g carbohydrate, 12g total fat (6g saturated), 1g fiber, 84mg cholesterol, 230mg sodium

deep-dish apple pie

This is the easiest apple pie you'll ever make—and we think one of the best! Tart Granny Smith apples are topped with a no-roll biscuitlike crust that's crisp on the outside and moist and tender inside.

active time 40 minutes plus cooling   **bake time** 1 hour 15 minutes
makes 12 servings

APPLE FILLING

6 pounds Granny Smith apples (about 12 large)

¾ cup sugar

⅓ cup all-purpose flour

2 tablespoons lemon juice

½ teaspoon cinnamon

BISCUIT CRUST

2 cups all-purpose flour

2 teaspoons baking powder

½ teaspoon salt

¼ cup plus 1 tablespoon sugar

4 tablespoons butter

1 large egg, beaten

⅔ cup plus 2 tablespoons heavy or whipping cream

each serving About 380 calories, 4g protein, 71g carbohydrate, 11g total fat (6g saturated), 5g fiber, 50mg cholesterol, 229mg sodium

1 Preheat oven to 400°F.

2 Prepare filling: Peel and core apples; cut each into 16 wedges. In large bowl, combine apples, sugar, flour, lemon juice, and cinnamon; toss to coat well. Spoon mixture into 13" by 9" baking dish; set aside.

3 Prepare crust: In medium bowl, mix flour, baking powder, salt, and ¼ cup sugar. With pastry blender or two knives used scissor-fashion, cut in butter until mixture resembles coarse crumbs. Stir in egg and ⅔ cup cream until blended.

4 With floured hands, shape dough into disk. Divide into 6 pieces; flatten each to about ½-inch thickness and arrange on top of apple mixture. (Dough will spread as it bakes.) Brush dough with remaining 2 tablespoons cream and sprinkle with remaining 1 tablespoon sugar.

5 Place sheet of foil underneath baking dish. Bake 35 minutes, then cover pie loosely with a tent of foil to prevent overbrowning. Continue baking until apples are tender when pierced with a knife, bubbles fill in the center, and crust is golden, about 40 minutes longer. Cool pie on wire rack 1 hour to serve warm, or cool completely to serve later.

blueberry cream pie

Make the most of in-season berries with this luscious dessert.

active time 25 minutes plus cooling and chilling   **bake time** 25 minutes
makes 10 servings

1 Prepare, bake, and cool pastry crust or deep-dish crust as recipe or label directs.

2 In 2-quart saucepan, mix milk, egg yolks, ¼ cup sugar, and 2 tablespoons cornstarch. Cook over medium heat, stirring, until mixture boils and thickens. Stir in vanilla and 1 tablespoon butter. Transfer custard to shallow dish; lay plastic wrap directly on surface to prevent skin from forming. Refrigerate 2 hours.

3 Meanwhile, in 3-quart saucepan, mix 1 cup berries with water and remaining ⅔ cup sugar and 3 tablespoons cornstarch. Heat to boiling over high heat. Cook 2 minutes to thicken, stirring. Stir in lemon juice and remaining 1 tablespoon butter; let cool. Stir in remaining 3 cups berries.

4 Spread custard in pie shell; top with berry mixture. Refrigerate until set, at least 3 hours.

Pastry for 9-Inch Pie (page 118), or frozen deep-dish piecrust, thawed

1¼ cups whole milk

2 egg yolks, beaten

¼ cup plus ⅔ cup sugar

5 tablespoons cornstarch

½ teaspoon vanilla extract

2 tablespoons butter (no substitutions)

4 cups blueberries

1 cup water

1 tablespoon fresh lemon juice

each serving About 245 calories, 3g protein, 39g carbohydrate, 10g total fat (3g saturated), 2g fiber, 53mg cholesterol, 145mg sodium

pecan pie
with bourbon crème

Maple syrup–drenched pecans are the sweet and sticky filling for this perfect holiday pie. A bourbon-infused whipped cream adds to the festive feeling.

active time 25 minutes plus cooling   **bake time** 45 minutes   **makes** 12 servings

1 Preheat oven to 350°F. In 3-quart saucepan, heat maple syrup, granulated sugar, and butter over medium heat until mixture boils. Reduce heat to medium-low and cook, stirring, 5 minutes.

2 In large bowl, with wire whisk, beat eggs slightly; slowly whisk in hot syrup mixture. Stir in vanilla.

3 Place unbaked crust on foil-lined cookie sheet to catch any overflow during baking. Arrange pecans evenly in bottom of crust. Pour syrup mixture over pecans.

4 Bake until filling is just set, 45 to 50 minutes. Cool pie on wire rack at least 1 hour.

5 To serve, in small bowl, with mixer on medium speed, beat cream with confectioners' sugar and bourbon until stiff peaks form; pass around to spoon on pie.

1 cup pure maple syrup

1 cup granulated sugar

4 tablespoons butter (no substitutions)

4 large eggs

1 tablespoon vanilla extract

Pastry for 9-Inch Pie (page 118), prepared through step 2, or frozen deep-dish piecrust, thawed

1½ cups pecan halves or large pecan pieces (6 ounces)

1 cup heavy or whipping cream

2 tablespoons confectioners' sugar

1 to 2 tablespoons bourbon

each serving About 420 calories, 4g protein, 43g carbohydrate, 26g total fat (10g saturated), 1g fiber, 109mg cholesterol, 140 mg sodium

easy eggnog pumpkin pie

Guests will love this festive twist on classic pumpkin pie.

active time 5 minutes plus cooling and chilling   **bake time** 1 hour
makes 12 servings

Pastry for 9-Inch Pie (page 118), prepared through step 2, or frozen deep-dish piecrust, thawed

1 can (15 ounces) pure pumpkin (not pumpkin-pie mix)

1¼ cups prepared eggnog

⅔ cup sugar

1½ teaspoons pumpkin-pie spice, plus additional for garnish

¼ teaspoon salt

3 large eggs

1 cup heavy cream

each serving About 165 calories, 3g protein, 23g carbohydrate, 7g total fat (3g saturated), 1g fiber, 69mg cholesterol, 150mg sodium

1 Prepare pastry or deep-dish crust as recipe or label directs.

2 Preheat oven to 375°F. In large bowl, with wire whisk, mix pumpkin, eggnog, sugar, pumpkin-pie spice, salt, and eggs until well blended. Place pie plate on foil-lined cookie sheet on oven rack; pour in pumpkin mixture (mixture will come up to almost top of crust).

3 Bake until filling puffs up around edges and center is just set but not puffed, 60 to 65 minutes. Cool completely on wire rack. Refrigerate until ready to serve.

4 In small bowl, with mixer on medium speed, beat cream until stiff peaks form. Garnish each serving of pie with whipped cream sprinkled with pumpkin-pie spice.

peach hand pies

These peachy-sweet turnovers are fun to eat. Everyone gets their own little pie.

active time 1 hour plus cooling **bake time** 18 minutes

makes 16 hand pies

1 In nonstick 12-inch skillet, melt butter over medium heat. In cup, mix cornstarch with ⅓ cup sugar. Stir peaches, sugar mixture, and salt into butter in skillet. Cook, stirring frequently, until peaches are very soft and mixture thickens and boils, 25 minutes. Boil 1 minute. Remove from heat; stir in lemon juice. Cool completely. (Refrigerate up to 24 hours.)

2 Preheat oven to 425°F. Prepare pastry as recipe directs.

3 On work surface, place 1 dough round and cut into quarters. Spoon 2 tablespoons filling in strip down center of each quarter, leaving about ¾ inch dough uncovered at each end. Fold dough over filling. With fork, press edges together to seal. Transfer to ungreased cookie sheet. Repeat with remaining dough and filling, placing 8 pies on each of two cookie sheets.

4 Brush tops of pies with egg; sprinkle with remaining 1 tablespoon sugar. With knife, cut 1-inch slit in top of each pie to vent steam during baking.

5 Bake pies until golden brown, 18 to 20 minutes, rotating cookie sheets between upper and lower oven racks halfway through. Cool completely on wire racks.

1 tablespoon butter or margarine

4 teaspoons cornstarch

⅓ cup plus 1 tablespoon sugar

2 pounds ripe peaches (about 4 large), unpeeled, pitted, and cut into ¾-inch pieces

⅛ teaspoon salt

1 tablespoon fresh lemon juice

4 recipes Pastry for 9-Inch Pie (page 118), prepared through step 1 and rolled into rounds

1 large egg, lightly beaten

each hand pie About 290 calories, 2g protein, 37g carbohydrate, 15g total fat (7g saturated), 1g fiber, 25mg cholesterol, 225mg sodium

apple-frangipane tart

This luscious tart makes a wonderful autumn dessert.

active time 35 minutes plus cooling **bake time** 1 hour 30 minutes
makes 12 servings

Pastry for 11-Inch Tart
(page 119), warm from
oven

1 tube or can (7 to 8
ounces) almond paste,
crumbled

4 tablespoons butter or
margarine, softened

½ cup sugar

¼ teaspoon salt

2 large eggs

¼ cup all-purpose flour

1¼ pounds Granny Smith
apples (about 3 medium)

¼ cup apricot jam

1 tablespoon amaretto
(almond-flavored liqueur)

each serving About 360
calories, 5g protein, 41g
carbohydrate, 21g total
fat (9g saturated), 2g fiber,
68mg cholesterol, 285mg
sodium

1 Prepare and bake tart shell as recipe directs.
2 While pastry bakes, in food processor with knife blade attached, pulse almond paste, butter, sugar, and salt until mixture is crumbly. Add eggs and pulse until smooth, scraping bowl with rubber spatula if necessary. (Tiny lumps may remain.) Add flour and pulse just until combined.
3 Peel, halve, and core apples; slice very thinly.
4 Remove tart shell from oven and allow to cool slightly. Leave oven set at 375°F.
5 Spoon almond filling into warm tart shell and spread evenly. Arrange apple slices over filling, closely overlapping in concentric circles. Bake until apples are tender when pierced with a knife, 1 hour to 1 hour and 10 minutes. Cool tart slightly on wire rack.
6 In 1-quart saucepan, heat jam and liqueur over low heat until jam melts, about 2 minutes. Press mixture through sieve into small bowl, then brush over warm apple slices. Finish cooling tart in pan on wire rack. Carefully remove side of pan and slide tart onto serving plate. Serve at room temperature or refrigerate up to 24 hours. If tart is refrigerated, let stand at room temperature at least 1 hour before serving.

grape and ginger tart

If seedless black grapes are available, add them to the mix along with the red and green ones for an extradramatic look.

active time 30 minutes plus cooling **bake time** 8 minutes
makes 10 servings

1 Prepare, bake, and cool crust as recipe directs.
2 In medium bowl, with wooden spoon, mix cream cheese, sour cream, brown sugar, and 3 tablespoons crystallized ginger until evenly blended. Spread filling evenly into cooled crust.
3 Place enough grape halves, cut side down, on top of filling to make a single layer. Scatter remaining grape halves over pie.
4 With pastry brush, carefully brush warm apple jelly over grapes and sprinkle with remaining 1 tablespoon slivered crystallized ginger. To serve, carefully remove side of pan. If not serving right away, cover and refrigerate, then let tart stand at room temperature 15 minutes before cutting.

Simple Crumb Crust (page 117), made with gingersnaps using 9-inch tart pan

1 package light cream cheese, or Neufchâtel (8 ounces)

¼ cup reduced-fat sour cream

2 tablespoons packed light brown sugar

4 tablespoons finely slivered or chopped crystallized ginger

2 cups seedless green and red grapes, each cut in half

2 tablespoons apple jelly, melted

each serving About 265 calories, 4g protein, 35g carbohydrate, 12g total fat (5g saturated), 1g fiber, 13mg cholesterol, 325mg sodium

mango tart

This tart takes a tropical turn with its lime pastry cream and sliced mango and kiwi.

active time 45 minutes plus chilling and cooling **bake time** 35 minutes
makes 8 servings

1¼ cups all-purpose flour

¼ cup confectioners' sugar

¼ teaspoon salt

10 tablespoons cold butter (no substitutions)

3 to 4 tablespoons ice water

1 cup whole milk

3 large egg yolks

⅓ cup granulated sugar

2 tablespoons cornstarch

1 teaspoon grated lime peel

2 mangoes, peeled and thinly sliced

1 slice peeled kiwifruit (optional)

1 In food processor with knife blade attached, combine flour, confectioners' sugar, and salt; pulse until blended. Cut up 8 tablespoons butter, add to bowl, and pulse until mixture resembles coarse meal. Add ice water, 1 tablespoon at a time, pulsing until moist clumps form. Shape dough into disk, wrap in plastic, and refrigerate until firm enough to roll, about 1 hour.

2 Preheat oven to 400°F. On lightly floured surface, with floured rolling pin, roll disk into 11-inch round. Transfer to 9-inch round tart pan with removable bottom. Press onto bottom and up side of pan. Trim dough level with rim of pan. Chill pastry 10 to 15 minutes to firm dough.

3 Line tart shell with foil and fill with pie weights or dry beans. Bake 20 minutes. Remove foil and weights and bake 15 minutes longer or until golden. (Cover rim with foil if browning too quickly.) If crust puffs during baking, gently press down with back of spoon. Cool in pan on wire rack, about 30 minutes.

4 Meanwhile, in 2-quart saucepan, heat milk to simmering on medium. In small bowl, whisk egg yolks and granulated sugar until blended. Mix in cornstarch until smooth. Whisking constantly, gradually pour half of simmering milk into yolk

mixture. Add yolk mixture to milk in saucepan and cook, whisking constantly to prevent lumping, until mixture boils and thickens, about 1 minute. Boil 1 minute, stirring. Remove saucepan from heat; stir in remaining 2 tablespoons butter and lime peel. Transfer pastry cream to small bowl; press plastic wrap directly onto surface to prevent skin from forming and refrigerate at least 1 hour.

5 Spread pastry cream evenly into baked tart shell. Arrange mango slices on top; place kiwifruit slice in center, if using. Remove pan side and place tart, still on base, on serving plate. If not serving right away, cover and refrigerate up to 2 hours.

each serving About 335 calories, 5g protein, 39g carbohydrate, 19g total fat (11g saturated), 2g fiber, 125mg cholesterol, 245mg sodium

cranberry almond tart

This sweet-tart dessert makes a pretty finale to a holiday meal.

active time 40 minutes plus cooling **bake time** 50 minutes
makes 10 servings

Pastry for 11-Inch Tart (page 119), warm from oven

½ cup almond paste (about 5 ounces)

1¼ cups sugar

½ cup butter or margarine (1 stick), softened

2 large eggs

3 tablespoons all-purpose flour

½ teaspoon grated orange peel

1 bag (12 ounces) cranberries (about 3 cups)

⅓ cup water

each serving About 315 calories, 4g protein, 45g carbohydrate, 14g total fat (7g saturated), 2g fiber, 69mg cholesterol, 170mg sodium

1 Prepare and bake pastry as recipe directs.

2 Reset oven to 350°F.

3 In food processor, with knife blade attached, process almond paste, ½ cup sugar, and butter until smooth. Add eggs and flour; process until mixed.

4 Fill hot tart shell with almond filling. Bake until filling is slightly puffed and golden, 20 to 25 minutes. Cool in pan on wire rack.

5 Meanwhile, in 2-quart saucepan, combine orange peel, 1 cup cranberries, remaining ¾ cup sugar, and water; heat over high heat until boiling. Reduce heat to medium-low; simmer 5 minutes until mixture thickens slightly and cranberries pop. Stir in remaining 2 cups cranberries. Set filling aside to cool.

6 When filling has cooled, remove side of tart pan and carefully slide tart crust onto serving plate. Spoon cranberry filling over almond filling.

chocolate caramel walnut tart

Rich creamy caramel, bittersweet chocolate, and toasty nuts join forces to create this luscious tart.

active time 40 minutes plus cooling and chilling   **bake time** 20 minutes
makes 12 servings

1 Prepare, bake, and cool pastry as recipe directs.

2 In heavy 3-quart saucepan, dissolve sugar in water over medium-high heat and cook, swirling pan occasionally, until syrup is amber in color, about 10 minutes. Remove from heat. Stir in ¾ cup cream until smooth caramel forms; stir in chocolate and butter until melted. Stir in chopped walnuts and vanilla.

3 Pour warm chocolate filling into cooled tart shell. Refrigerate until set, at least 3 hours. Remove side of pan. Just before serving, in medium bowl, with mixer on medium speed, beat remaining 1 cup cream until stiff peaks form. Garnish tart with whipped cream and walnut halves.

Pastry for 11-Inch Tart (page 119)

1 cup sugar

¼ cup water

1¾ cups heavy cream

8 squares (8 ounces) bittersweet chocolate, chopped

2 tablespoons butter or margarine

2 cups walnuts (8 ounces), lightly toasted (page 11) and chopped, plus additional halves for garnish

2 teaspoons vanilla extract

each serving About 505 calories, 6g protein, 42g carbohydrate, 38g total fat (16g saturated), 3g fiber, 48mg cholesterol, 160mg sodium

raspberry ganache tart

A rich, buttery crust that melts in your mouth like shortbread is topped with a bittersweet-chocolate filling and a sprinkling of raspberries.

active time 30 minutes plus chilling and cooling **bake time** 28 minutes
makes 12 servings

1 Preheat oven to 325°F. In medium bowl, with fork, combine flour, cornstarch, confectioners' sugar, and salt. Cut ½ cup butter into pieces. With pastry blender or two knives used scissor-fashion, cut butter and 1 teaspoon vanilla into flour mixture until fine crumbs form and mixture is just moist enough to hold together. Pat dough into 9-inch round tart pan with removeable bottom.

2 Place sheet of plastic wrap over dough and smooth dough evenly over bottom and up side of pan. Remove and discard plastic wrap. With fork, prick shell at ½-inch intervals; place in freezer 10 minutes or refrigerator 30 minutes to firm crust.

3 Bake until golden, 28 to 30 minutes. Cool completely in pan on wire rack.

4 Meanwhile, in 2-quart saucepan, heat cream with remaining 3 tablespoons butter to boiling over medium-high heat. Remove from heat; add chocolates and, with wire whisk, whisk until melted and smooth. Whisk in remaining ½ teaspoon vanilla.

5 Spread hot ganache into cooled crust. Sprinkle with raspberries. Refrigerate until chilled and firm, about 1 hour. If tart must be refrigerated more than 1 hour, let stand at room temperature 30 minutes before serving.

¾ cup all-purpose flour

⅓ cup cornstarch

⅓ cup confectioners' sugar

⅛ teaspoon salt

½ cup plus 3 tablespoons cold butter, cut up (no substitutions)

1½ teaspoons vanilla extract

½ cup heavy cream

7 squares (7 ounces) semisweet chocolate, coarsely chopped

1 square (1 ounce) unsweetened chocolate, coarsely chopped

½ pint raspberries (about 1½ cups)

each serving About 280 calories, 2g protein, 25g carbohydrate, 21g total fat (13g saturated), 2g fiber, 42mg cholesterol, 138mg sodium

fruit tartlets

For elegant individual desserts, make up plates of four tartlets each. The color combination of kiwifruit and strawberries always feels festive.

active time 45 minutes plus cooling **bake time** 15 minutes
makes 24 tartlets

Pastry for 9-Inch Tart (page 119), prepared through step 3

1 container whipped cream cheese (8 ounces)

3 tablespoons sugar

1 tablespoon milk

¾ teaspoon vanilla extract

2 cups assorted fruit, such as sliced kiwifruit, halved strawberries, canned mandarin-orange sections, and small seedless red and green grape halves

Mint leaves for garnish (optional)

each tartlet About 100 calories, 1g protein, 8g carbohydrate, 7g total fat (4g saturated), 0g fiber, 18mg cholesterol, 80mg sodium

1 Preheat oven to 425°F. Divide chilled dough in half. With hands, roll each half into 12-inch rope; cut each rope into twelve 1-inch pieces. Press each piece of dough evenly into 24 mini muffin-pan cups to make mini pastry shells. Prick each several times with toothpick. Bake until golden, about 15 minutes. Cool in pans on wire rack 5 minutes. Carefully remove from pans; cool completely on wire rack.

2 Meanwhile, in small bowl, with fork, beat cream cheese, sugar, milk, and vanilla until blended. Refrigerate until ready to serve.

3 Fill each tartlet shell with about 2 teaspoons filling; top with fruit. Garnish with mint leaves, if desired.

simple crumb crust

A basic cookie-crumb crust—three ways.

active time 10 minutes   **bake time** 8 minutes
makes one 9- inch crust

1 Preheat oven to 375°F. In medium bowl, with fork, stir crumbs and sugar with melted butter until evenly blended and moistened. With hand, press mixture onto bottom and up side of 9-inch pie plate, springform pan, or tart pan with removable bottom.

2 Bake 8 to 10 minutes. Cool on wire rack.

how many cookies do you need?

Generally, you need 1½ cups cookie crumbs to make a 9-inch piecrust. That's about . . .

    10 graham crackers (the full rectangles)
    30 gingersnaps (2-inch size)
    45 vanilla wafers (1½-inch size)
    27 chocolate wafers (2½-inch size)

1½ cups fine cookie crumbs such as graham crackers, gingersnaps, or vanilla wafers

2 tablespoons sugar

5 tablespoons butter or margarine, melted

each ¹⁄₁₀ graham cracker crust About 115 calories, 1g protein, 12g carbohydrate, 7g total fat (4g saturated), 0g fiber, 16mg cholesterol, 135mg sodium

each ¹⁄₁₀ gingersnap crust About 140 calories, 1g protein, 17g carbohydrate, 8g total fat (4g saturated), 0g fiber, 16mg cholesterol, 184mg sodium

each ¹⁄₁₀ vanilla wafer crust About 185 calories, 1g protein, 21g carbohydrate, 11g total fat (5g saturated), 1g fiber, 16mg cholesterol, 136mg sodium

pastry for 9-inch pie

Use this foolproof basic pie dough as the foundation for as many pies as you can dream up.

active time 25 minutes plus chilling **bake time** 25 minutes
makes one 9-inch crust

1¼ cups all-purpose flour

¼ teaspoon salt

4 tablespoons cold butter or margarine (½ stick), cut up

2 tablespoons vegetable shortening

4 to 6 tablespoons ice water

each ¹⁄₁₀ pastry About 125 calories, 2g protein, 13g carbohydrate, 7g total fat (4g saturated), 0g fiber, 12mg cholesterol, 105mg sodium

1 In large bowl, mix flour and salt. With pastry blender or two knives used scissor-fashion, cut in butter and shortening until mixture resembles coarse crumbs. Stir ice water, 1 tablespoon at a time, into flour mixture, mixing well after each addition until dough is just moist enough to hold together. With hands, shape dough into disk. Wrap disk in plastic and refrigerate until firm enough to roll, about 30 minutes.

2 On lightly floured surface, with floured rolling pin, roll dough into round 1½ inches larger in diameter than inverted 9-inch pie plate. Ease dough into pie plate; trim edge, leaving 1-inch overhang. Fold overhang under; bring up over pie-plate rim and pinch to form high decorative edge.

3 Preheat oven to 375°F. Line pie shell with foil or parchment and fill with pie weights or dry beans. Bake pastry until beginning to set, 12 to 14 minutes. Remove foil with weights and continue baking until golden, 13 to 15 minutes longer. Cool in pan on wire rack.

tart pastry

A perfect tart crust in two sizes—11- or 9-inch.

active time 10 minutes plus chilling **bake time** 30 minutes
makes one 11- or 9- inch tart shell

1 In large bowl, mix flour and salt. With pastry blender or two knives used scissor-fashion, cut in butter and shortening until mixture resembles coarse crumbs.

2 Sprinkle in 3 to 4 tablespoons ice water for 11-inch tart (2 to 3 tablespoons for 9-inch), 1 tablespoon at a time, mixing lightly with fork after each addition, until dough is just moist enough to hold together.

3 Shape dough into disk. Wrap disk in plastic and refrigerate 30 minutes or up to overnight. If chilled overnight, let stand at room temperature 30 minutes before rolling out.

4 On lightly floured surface, with floured rolling pin, roll dough into 14-inch round (12 inches for 9-inch pan). Ease dough into 11-inch (or 9-inch) round tart pan with removable bottom. Fold overhang in and press against side of tart pan to form a rim $1/8$ inch above edge of pan. Refrigerate 15 minutes to firm pastry slightly.

5 Preheat oven to 375°F. Line tart shell with foil and fill with pie weights or dry beans. Bake 20 minutes; remove foil with weights and bake until golden, 8 to 10 minutes longer. Cool in pan on wire rack.

FOR 11-INCH TART

1½ cups all-purpose flour

½ teaspoon salt

½ cup cold butter or margarine (1 stick), cut up

2 tablespoons shortening

FOR 9-INCH TART

1 cup all-purpose flour

¼ teaspoon salt

6 tablespoons cold butter or margarine, cut up

1 tablespoon shortening

each $1/12$ pastry (for 11-inch tart): About 145 calories, 2g protein, 13g carbohydrate, 10g total fat (5g saturated), 21mg cholesterol, 175mg sodium

each $1/8$ pastry (for 9-inch tart) About 150 calories, 2g protein, 13g carbohydrate, 10g total fat (6g saturated), 23mg cholesterol, 160mg sodium

volume equivalents

SMALL VOLUME

TABLESPOONS	CUPS	FLUID OUNCES
1 tablespoon = 3 teaspoons		½ fluid ounce
2 tablespoons	⅛ cup	1 fluid ounce
4 tablespoons	¼ cup	2 fluid ounces
5 tablespoons + 1 teaspoon	⅓ cup	2⅔ fluid ounces
6 tablespoons	⅜ cup	3 fluid ounces
8 tablespoons	½ cup	4 fluid ounces
10 tablespoons +2 teaspoons	⅔ cup	5⅓ fluid ounces
12 tablespoons	¾ cup	6 fluid ounces
14 tablespoons	⅞ cup	7 fluid ounces
16 tablespoons	1 cup	8 fluid ounces

LARGER VOLUME

CUPS	FLUID OUNCES	PINTS/QUARTS/GALLONS
1 cup	8 fluid ounces	½ pint
2 cups	16 fluid ounces	1 pint
3 cups	24 fluid ounces	1½ pints = ¾ quart
4 cups	32 fluid ounces	2 pints = 1 quart
6 cups	48 fluid ounces	3 pints = 1½ quarts
8 cups	64 fluid ounces	2 quarts = ½ gallon
16 cups	128 fluid ounces	4 quarts = 1 gallon

pan volumes

PAN SIZE	APPROXIMATE VOLUME
2½" by 1½" muffin-pan cup	½ cup
8½" by 4½" by 2½" loaf pan	6 cups
9" by 5" by 3" loaf pan	8 cups
8" by 8" by 1½" baking pan	6 cups
9" by 9" by 1½" baking pan	8 cups
9" by 1" pie plate	4 cups
11" by 7" by 1½" baking pan	8 cups
13" by 9" by 2" baking pan	15 cups
15½" by 10½" by 1" jelly-roll pan	16 cups

MEASURING PANS

To get an accurate measurement of your bakeware, follow the guidelines below.

pan volume Using a measuring cup, fill a baking pan to the rim with water, just short of overflowing, and count the number of cups required. This is the cup volume of the pan. If you have a pan with a removeable bottom, substitute granulated sugar for water.

pan sizes With a ruler, measure the length and width of the pan across its top from one inside edge to the opposite inside edge. Holding the ruler perpendicular to the pan, measure the depth of the inside of the pan from the bottom to the rim.

metric equivalents

The recipes in this book use the standard U.S. method for measuring liquid and dry or solid ingredients (teaspoons, tablespoons, and cups). The information on the following charts is provided to help cooks outside the United States successfully use these recipes. All equivalents are approximate.

METRIC EQUIVALENTS FOR DIFFERENT TYPES OF INGREDIENTS
A standard cup measure of a dry or solid ingredient will vary in weight depending on the type of ingredient. A standard cup of liquid is the same volume for any type of liquid. Use the following chart when converting standard cup measures to grams (weight) or milliliters (volume).

STANDARD CUP	FINE POWDER (E.G., FLOUR)	GRAIN (E.G., RICE)	GRANULAR (E.G., GRANULATED SUGAR)	LIQUID SOLIDS (E.G., BUTTER)	LIQUID (E.G., MILK)
1	140 g	150 g	190 g	200 g	240 ml
¾	105 g	113 g	143 g	150 g	180 ml
⅔	93 g	100 g	125 g	133 g	160 ml
½	70 g	75 g	95 g	100 g	120 ml
⅓	47 g	50 g	63 g	67 g	80 ml
¼	35 g	38 g	48 g	50 g	60 ml
⅛	18 g	19 g	24 g	25 g	30 ml

USEFUL EQUIVALENTS FOR DRY INGREDIENTS BY WEIGHT
(To convert ounces to grams, multiply the number of ounces by 30.)

1 oz	=	²⁄₁₆ lb	=	30 g
4 oz	=	¼ lb	=	120 g
8 oz	=	½ lb	=	240 g
12 oz	=	¾ lb	=	360 g
16 oz	=	1 lb	=	480 g

USEFUL EQUIVALENTS FOR LIQUID INGREDIENTS BY VOLUME

¼ tsp	=							1 ml		
½ tsp	=							2 ml		
1 tsp	=							5 ml		
3 tsp	=	1 tblsp	=			½ fl oz	=	15 ml		
		2 tblsp	=	⅛ cup	=	1 fl oz	=	30 ml		
		4 tblsp	=	¼ cup	=	2 fl oz	=	60 ml		
		5⅓ tblsp	=	⅓ cup	=	3 fl oz	=	80 ml		
		8 tblsp	=	½ cup	=	4 fl oz	=	120 ml		
		10⅔ tblsp	=	⅔ cup	=	5 fl oz	=	160 ml		
		12 tblsp	=	¾ cup	=	6 fl oz	=	180 ml		
		16 tblsp	=	1 cup	=	8 fl oz	=	240 ml		
		1 pt	=	2 cups	=	16 fl oz	=	480 ml		
		1 qt	=	4 cups	=	32 fl oz	=	960 ml		
						33 fl oz	=	1000 ml	=	1 L

USEFUL EQUIVALENTS FOR COOKING/OVEN TEMPERATURES

	FARENHEIT	CELSIUS	GAS MARK
Freeze water	32°F	0°C	
Room temperature	68°F	20°C	
Boil water	212°F	100°C	
Bake	325°F	160°C	3
	350°F	180°C	4
	375°F	190°C	5
	400°F	200°C	6
	425°F	220°C	7
	450°F	230°C	8
Broil			Grill

USEFUL EQUIVALENTS FOR LENGTH

(To convert inches to centimeters, multiply the number of inches by 2.5.)

1 in	=					2.5 cm		
6 in	=	½ ft	=			15 cm		
12 in	=	1 ft	=			30 cm		
36 in	=	3 ft	=	1 yd	=	90 cm		
40 in	=					100 cm	=	1 m

index

photography credits

Sang An: 35, 66, 71, 97
James Baigrie: 54
Getty Images: Rosemary Calvert, 13; Food Collection, 14, 19; Food Photography Eising, 20; Alison Miksch, 57; Radius Images, 18, Ann Stratton: 39
Brian Hagiwara: 8, 17, 91, 100, 106, 114
iStockphoto: 22; VisualCommunications, 11
Frances Janisch: 111
Ray Kachatorian: 59
Yunhee Kim: 22
Rita Maas: 48, 77
Kate Mathis: 2
Steven Mark Needham: 10, 31, 75, 96, 109
Alan Richardson: p. 53, 105
Stockfood: Valerie Janssen, 6
Ann Stratton: 29, 37, 43, 63, 92
Studio D: Philip Friedman, 7
Mark Thomas: 45

Front Cover: Getty Images, Deborah Ory
Spine: Getty Images, Alexandra Grablewski
Back Cover: Stockfood,Valerie Janssen (top), Brian Hagiwara (bottom)

recipe for

from the kitchen of

recipe for

from the kitchen of

recipe for

from the kitchen of

recipe for

from the kitchen of

recipe for

from the kitchen of

recipe for

from the kitchen of

recipe for

from the kitchen of

recipe for

from the kitchen of